# MODI

## THE MAHAAN!?

### India's PM till 2034!

## Krishnaraja M Manjunatha

**NEXUS STORIES PUBLICATION®**

Surat, Gujarat, India.

Title – **Modi The Mahaan!?**

First Published by Nexus Stories Publication 2024

**Copyright © Krishnaraja M Manjunatha 2024**

**All Rights Reserved.**

**ISBN # 978-81-971478-4-5**



Publication

Nexus Stories Publication®, Surat (Gujarat), Bhārata
www.nexus-stories.com # +91 87800 80718

# MODI-THE MAHAAN!?
## INDIA'S PM TILL 2034!

No leader in any democratic country across the globe has captivated the mind-space of their countrymen the way Narendra Modi has, in the world's largest democracy-India. And, it shall only increase year after year.

In this quick read and his trademark "free-flowing style", Krishnaraja M Manjunatha, a journalist-cum-critic who has studied Modi for over 25 years closely, and who resigned from a coveted civil services position for his passion for journalism, is about to decipher why and how Modi trounced all till date and shall continue as the Prime Minister till 2034 and what all transformation he shall unleash to make Bharat, Vishwaguru!

**Krishnaraja M Manjunatha**

**"Narendra Modi** shall be India's Prime Minister till 2034".

When I told this to a fellow journalist, a Modi-baiter, he laughed off.

I was serious. I had my way of understanding, analyzing, and deciphering Modi.

"BJP's party constitution has made it a point to retire their political leaders at the age of 75 years. This was brought into effect on great leaders like Advani and MM Joshi too. It's Narendra Modi only who brought in this rule after becoming the Prime Minister in 2014", he argued.

I didn't blink.

"Modi has one critical record to break. And, only he will be able to break that record. Till then, he shall not retire"

My journalist friend raised his eyebrow.

"Jawaharlal Nehru, a Congressman, has the record of longest-serving prime minister of India at 16 years 286 days. Modi requires seven more years as PM to break that record. That means, the year 2031."

I posted my logic.

He was more perturbed, "But Modi is 73 now, and he would be 80 years then, and as per his party constitution, he can't continue after 75 years".

I said, "Wait and see."

>>>

**It's March 2024.** The Lok Sabha election schedule has just been announced.

All pre-poll surveys have declared that Modi, BJP, and NDA are back in power for the third consecutive term. Now, the debate is what the victory margin would be.

Modi has set a high target this time- 370 seats for the BJP and 400 for his alliance NDA, out of 543 seats!

What's he up to?

But the media, the BJP cadre, and most voters believe it's possible.

Because, in the 2014 and 2019 Lok Sabha elections, Modi had wielded magic and had reached the magic numbers he had predicted.

**Modi wants all or none.**

That's the audacity he had shown or clarity he had expressed when he was chosen as the Chief Minister of Gujarat for the first time in 2001.

>>>

**It was** in 2001, I was leading the charge at India's largest television/news network, ETV, as a loyal lieutenant of Sri Ramoji Raogaru, Honourable Chairman of that Eenadu Group whom I revere as my only Guru.

Going by the political standards, Modi was young to be a Chief Minister at 49 years. Going by the media standards, with the position I was in, I was very young at 30 years!

That's how I know Modi, know about him, and have been closely studying him since then.

One interesting thing then. ETV being a pan India television/news network, whenever there was a big *neta* or a celebrity, we used to have interviews with them both in their regional language and Hindi or English. When Modi assumed charge as the Chief Minister, we didn't even bother to take his interview in Hindi. It was just in Gujarati.

Whoever considered him insignificant or just a regional satrap was wrong. But I didn't. As I was planning and coordinating the Gujarat events and Assembly elections in 2001 and 2002- everything revolving around Modi, I could feel something big was brewing around him. And, he would turn any and every opportunity to his advantage.

Just taste this. He was not even a MLA when he became the Chief Minister. He was the first time MP when he became the Prime Minister. Since 2001, from the days of active politics, he hasn't lost a single election under his leadership be it Gujarat Assembly elections or Parliament elections.

Isn't it amazing in a multi-state, multi-lingual, multi-religious, multi-cultural, and too-diverse nation such as Bharat?

>>>

**Modi is** an enigma. Modi is a phenomenon. Modi is a maverick. Modi is a meticulous planner. Modi is an expert in springing surprises. Modi is a disruptor. Modi is Mahaan!?
Mahaan followed by! and?

(!) Exclamation and excitement to his admirers and *bhakts* (worshippers). (?) Question mark and anxiety to his baiters and opponents.

**Modi doesn't let anything and anyone go. That's his trait.**

Despite being the Prime Minister for two terms totaling ten years with an absolute majority on both occasions which is a rarity in the Indian polity since 1989, Modi has some political things unfulfilled yet- breaking Nehru's record as the longest serving Prime Minister, bringing BJP to power in all states of India, and making India Congress-*mukt.*

For that, he requires two more terms. Period.

Yes. He has also set high economic, social, and national targets.

- Making India the third largest economy by 2027; the second largest economy by 2037; a fully developed nation, and possibly, the world's largest economy by 2047, when India completes its 100 years of Independence.
- He is aware that Casteism and Communalism are dangerous to the unity of India. He wants to mitigate them or eliminate them.
- He wants every Indian to have the best amenities- be it LPG (Ujwala scheme), education (NEP), health (Swacch Bharat and Ayushman Bharat, clean, tap drinking water), electricity, internet, and adequate opportunities. There has been considerable progress in these areas too but for the burgeoning population, it's inadequate. He wants to do more in these areas.

- He understands the power of a strong military and has always kept it as a top priority.
- Bringing back India's glory and making it VISHWAGURU (The World's Leader/Teacher).
- There's a secret wish or thinking going on within the top circles of Modi- to take up interlinking of rivers across India that would reduce droughts and floods and make every part of India water-surplus, the way he did across the parched lands of Gujarat.

He also understands the enormity of this project and the huge costs it incurs and hence, might have pushed it further. Who knows after 2034, after retiring from active politics, he might just head this mega project and make it a reality by 2047, the 100th year of India's independence.

Believe me. He thinks very deeply and plans long.

Once he does all these, what else he would be? MAHAAN!.

And, the BJP Government at the Centre after Modi, might replace the pre-independence hero "Mahatma" with Independent India's hero "Mahaan" or "Maharshi"!

>>>

**I love** journalism so much that I gave up a coveted Karnataka state civil services position to pursue my passion and am on the way toward building a pan-India, top-notch integrated media brand/network.

Yes. I am proud, indeed very proud to be a journalist. A journalist needs to be unbiased, neutral, and objective, and so do I. A journalist has to report and present facts as they are, without adding spice. Those facts, if they are good for the society and the nation, need to be reported too, as they are, more so, not through his prism but from the general public point of view.

Journalists do admonish. But they appreciate good things too. Be it Ratan Tata, Sachin Tendulkar, or Rajinikanth- their goodness and accomplishments are indeed appreciated. Why ignore a good politician or his good deeds?

It's also a matter of curiosity and learning to understand and present how and why TATA has maintained its legacy, how Jio became No.1 in the Indian telecom market in a matter of a few months, and why the Indians couldn't build a brand like Apple, Google, Microsoft, Facebook, etc.

I belong to that category of journalists- inquisitive, unbiased, presenting bad as well as good acts as they are.

My school of journalism has always been issue-based and never on personal likes and dislikes.

Personality-based stories are different though. Be it Dhirubhai, Narayanamurthy, Dhoni or Modi provides us with several revelations, insights, and learnings.

I seriously study how Modi could become such a phenomenon or how the BJP has become the world's largest political party and is also becoming all-pervasive in India.

No one is perfect. So is Modi. But in the world's largest democracy, and that too in the era of social media, where everything spreads like wildfire if the wide majority of the people are electing him again and again means he must be close to perfection or better than others.

However, I am penning this book, not just as a journalist but also as a student of Management. Any student of any sort of Management- political management, personality management, business management, health management, competition management, marketing management, team management, life management, communications management, or even war management- by studying Modi closely, can gain a lot of insights and learn strategies.

>>>

**Modi wants all or none.**

That's what he told the top BJP leadership including stalwarts such as Vajpayee and Advani, way back in 2001, when he was asked to become a Deputy Chief Minister to the ailing and failing Chief Minister of Gujarat, Keshubhai Patel.

Anyone in Modi's position then who was not even an MLA and was not in the government but in the party would have lapped up that opportunity. But he said no.

Modi as a *karyakarta* had won Gujarat for the BJP. It's his toil at various levels for close to 20 years that had catapulted the BJP to power there. After BJP came to power and Keshubhai Patel had become the Chief Minister, frustrated with power games and fratricidal wars, Modi stayed aloof for a few years. Later, at the insistence of the national leaders, he moved to the BJP national office in New Delhi.

The ground reports in Gujarat in the late 1990s indicated that the BJP was slipping under Keshubhai Patel. Bhuj earthquake relief was poorly managed and the people were upset. The top BJP leadership had high expectations from Gujarat. Having known Modi's connections in Gujarat and his contributions to the success of the BJP in Gujarat, the top leadership insisted that he become Deputy Chief Minister to a powerful Chief Minister coming from a powerful caste.

In India, certain positions, more so, political positions, are "inherited" i.e. through ascribed status- through ancestral lineage like that of Rahul Gandhi or having been born in a dominant caste such as Keshubhai Patel in Gujarat.

Patel community is a very dominant community in Gujarat- numerically, socially, economically, educationally and politically.

Modi was born in a "contrasting" community or caste-Modh-Ghanchi, weak on all counts.

Caste is a watertight compartment. Each caste works in silos and acts as "pressure groups and vested interest groups". It's very difficult for a person of a weaker caste to raise even a voice before a person of a dominant caste. Getting into politics and emerging victorious is a far-fetched thing. Even today, in 2024, the main criterion while selecting a candidate is caste. Imagine what it would have been in the 1990s.

For Vajpayee as the Prime Minister and Advani as the party's *numero uno* leader, Gujarat was too important. They had to save the party and power there. But they were not prepared to antagonize a powerful leader

Keshubhai and his powerful caste, which had become the core of the BJP support in Gujarat.

They worked out a compromise formula- ailing, trailing Keshubhai to continue as CM and Modi to be brought in as Deputy Chief Minister to manage governance.

Modi knew its repercussions. He will not be allowed to deliver. So, he denied politely but firmly.

The situation was turning from bad to worse. The BJP's top leadership was compelled to replace Keshubhai with Modi.

Modi was a novice. Modi was also very much aware of the inherent limitations in the form of caste or financial resources. Every senior leader was about to treat him so. But he was not to allow that to happen.

Six things came to his aid:

1. His hard work.
2. To build a unique "Gujarat model of governance and development".
3. Strategic thinking and meticulous planning.
4. Dealing with and through efficient bureaucrats, and mandating MLAs to be with their voters.
5. A few devout followers the foremost being Amit Shah.
6. Of course, direct connection with national leaders.

He took up the earthquake relief on a war footing. Despite internal hurdles by the powerful gang of politicians, he started implementing things at an amazing pace and precision.

Still, during his initial months as CM, he lost three Assembly by-elections on a spree. Keshubhai and his loyal MLAs had rebelled.

Then followed a year-long turmoil- the Godhra train fire accident, communal riots, charges of him being complicit, Vajpayee calling him to follow "Raja Dharma", and non-stop vilification by the media and the Opposition.

Modi had become a person of "national and international attention". "India's secular values are under threat", screeched the media and the Opposition.

Vajpayee, a moderate face of the BJP and with the compulsion of allies in the national government, was under intense pressure. Under relentless attack from all quarters, Modi offered to resign at the party's national meet. Vajpayee would have happily accepted but for the intervention of Advani and Arun Jaitley and an old ally Shiv Sena's Bal Thackeray.

There was another angle that was developing parallelly. The Hindus, who long felt sidelined and subjugated in their motherland, saw a hero in Modi. He had become a symbol of Hindu resurrection to crores of Hindus across India- The Hindu Hruday Samrat like Chhatrapati Shivaji. Shiv Sena's Bal Thackeray, Vishwa Hindu Parishad, RSS stood firm with him.

What UP's Yogi Adityanath is today in 2024 for the hardcore Hindus from across India, Modi was the same in 2002.

Besides, Modi's administrative skills and control and vision of a "new Gujarat" had earned appreciation.

Despite continuous vilification by the media and the opposition, the people of Gujarat elected him and the BJP in the 2002 Assembly elections with a thumping majority.

The victory procession that started then has continued unabated.

He had proven caste and wealth are no hindrances to political victory if someone has character, performance, and merit. Still, with the political acumen that he has, he also does a lot of social engineering and gets the winning combination of social groups (castes)

>>>

**Modi and** the Indian Muslims- a very complex thing to decipher. This has been the most critical discourse throughout Modi's career.

Modi was born and brought up in Gujarat. He was also its Chief Minister thrice. The state's capital city is Gandhinagar, and its twin city is Ahmedabad.

Changing the name of a city has been a political game in most states in India. While some name-changes have been for historical and linguistic re-assertiveness, some have been for religious re-assertions. Allahabad was changed to Prayagraj and Faizabad to Ayodhya in Uttar Pradesh recently. The Maharashtra Government renamed Aurangabad as Chatrapati Sambhajinagar and Osmanabad as Dharashiv.

Modi is regarded as the "Hindu Hruday Samrat" of the independent India. Still, he didn't rename a prominent city in his home state- Ahmedabad.

Why? Modi has never answered this. Yet, I would like to decipher a bit of his mind on this.

Ahmedabad reminds the Hindus of "foreign invasion and assaults", and he lets it keep reminding them so that they are "beware" of it.

Another reason could be that he had already been discredited as a "Muslim-hater", and didn't want to further propagate that impression or image.

Or, changing a city's name is too small a thing in his overall game plan.

Is Modi a Hindu protector? Or a Muslim-hater?

Modi had made headlines in September 2011 for declining to put on a skull cap during his Sadbhavana (goodwill) fast in Ahmedabad, offered by a Muslim cleric. Instead, he accepted a green chadar from Maulavi Sayed Imam, which he draped around his shoulders. Modi emphasized later that Mahatma Gandhi, Sardar Patel, or Jawaharlal Nehru never wore a skull cap and it is not necessarily the symbol of unity.

Nevertheless, Modi was aware of the mistake Advani had committed by profusely admiring "India-divider" and Pakistan's founder Mohammed Ali Jinnah.

He was also aware of the mistake Vajpayee committed by "overpampering" Pakistan and its premier Pervez Musharaf, going "too liberal" during his Prime Ministership and not taking up the BJP's core promises.

These mistakes by such architects of the BJP had antagonized their core Hindu supporters and cadre and had cost them dearly. Modi measures every word and act and assesses its *pros* and *cons* in split seconds. It's to the credit of Modi that he has never committed a "slip of the tongue" or *gaffe.*

On the contrary, whoever Muslim leader has seen Modi, met Modi, and has worked with Modi or done business with Modi is of a different opinion. They say he doesn't discriminate in the government benefits and schemes.

Most of the Bohra Muslims in Gujarat are admirers of Modi. Why?

Bohras are very devout Muslims, are well-educated, and are in various businesses. They are peace-loving too. They have never allowed anyone to treat them as a mere vote bank. They treat religion as a private matter and well understand the political, social, and economic dynamics. They accommodate others and get accommodated by others.

Modi doesn't discriminate between the citizens, though he does not give the Muslims equal space in polity or bring them into his close circle of strategy and decision-making, at least till now. This might change in the days to come.

If one recalls Modi visiting the dressing room of the Indian cricket team post-defeat in the World Cup final 2023, he called Mohammed Shami, the highest wicket-taker with the same affection as the other players. "*Kya* Shami, *Bahut badiya kiya*" (Shami, you did great), and hugged him tight.

"Sabka Saath Sabka Vishwas Sabka Vikas" (With everyone, With everyone's trust and For everyone's progress) has been the mantra of Modi to rechange whatever image he has had or he is doing everything to Muslims too, genuinely.

Let's take triple talaq which has been badly affecting Muslim women. While most Islamic countries have banned this practice, in India it continued. Political parties didn't want to antagonize this influential pan-India "vote bank" dictated by Maulvis and dominated by men. However, Modi went ahead and banned it.

Abrogation of Article 370 was another major step. It had kept Jammu & Kashmir the only state in India with a majority Muslim population "virtually separate" from mainstream India. Whatever happened in Kashmir was projected as a pan-India Muslim phenomenon.

Understandably, the abrogation of Article 370 has been one of the main planks of RSS and the BJP. But it is also true that Article 370 had come as a block to the "unification of India" and the real development of Jammu & Kashmir.

Another contentious issue between the Hindus/ the BJP and the Muslims was the Ayodhya Ram Janmabhoomi issue. It kept burning and dividing these communities for decades. Even this has been amicably resolved. A big feat for Modi and the long-term amity, unity, and progress of India.

Modi openly advocated reaching out to Pasmanda Muslims, who are the most backward sections among the Muslims and has brought out some special schemes to uplift them. They are taking note of it.

Modi's earlier Home Minister and now, the Defence Minister, Rajnath Singh, on several occasions, has admired the Indian Muslims for their patriotism and has said that those falling prey to Islamic terrorism and fundamentalism are very few.

One can see the bonding and bonhomie between Modi and the leaders of Islamic nations including UAE and Bangladesh. One should note that he didn't make a single comment even when the Taliban took over Afghanistan and has been extending humanitarian assistance.

Only Pakistan is "no" to him in the Islamic world, more so, after the Pulwama attack.

It's to his credit that a beautiful Hindu temple was built in UAE, for the first time. In his recent address in UAE, one could see several Arab leaders seated in the first row to listen to Modi!

This is the main concern of the Opposition parties. Modi has already occupied the minds and souls of most Hindus. In case the Muslims too start accepting him and the BJP, then whatever space the opposition parties are left with, is gone!

Statistics show there's also a gradual shift of the Muslims, more so women and the youth towards Modi and the BJP. They are silent though. If it had not been so, BJP couldn't have got a massive mandate in the last Uttar Pradesh Assembly elections.

As more and more Muslims become the beneficiaries of the Modi government and as the most contentious issues between the Hindus and Muslims are getting resolved, the Muslims' votes shall only increase for the BJP.

**"India *Jannat* *hain!*"** (India is heaven!).

This is what a young Muslim from Kerala who worked in Dubai said while we both were awaiting a return flight to Bengaluru.

Muslims of India might go elsewhere to work like Hindus, more so, in the Gulf nations but citizenship there is hard to come by. They may earn in Dirhams and happily send some good money to their family back in India. But their souls feel the beauty and diversity of real India.

Real India has a place for all religions and there's complete harmony. If someone still has a doubt, he should watch a live cricket match and see for himself the naturality of the relationship between Hindu and Muslim players. What you see in a cricket stadium is what exists in the day-to-day lives of common Indians- Hindus and Muslims.

Modi and his government are clear- Do not disrespect other religions but do not allow anyone to meddle with India's core religion Hinduism or the nation. Join the mainstream, play your part in nation-building, and be a part of the collective progress.

Nevertheless, there have been stray incidents that cause occasional discord. They are going to decrease and disappear in the years to come as both the communities by and large, across India, are coming to terms with changes in polity as well as the society.

The Hindus had a feeling of "invaded" pre-independence and "suppressed" post-independence. The Hindus also felt that the Muslims were appeased by other parties. With the rise of the BJP and more so, Modi, the Hindus feel liberated. Besides, the hardcore BJP cadre's key demands of the Abrogation of Article 370 applicable to J&K and Ayodhya Ram Mandir have been fulfilled. Another demand for the Uniform Civil Code is being implemented at the level of states. Their minds are at ease now.

The Muslims on the other hand, felt threatened due to the rise of the BJP. The Muslims have realized that the Hindus are the actual inhabitants of Bharat, and have suffered from "the deprived" feeling for a long time that needs to be assuaged and accommodated. Some Muslims have also started to admit that their lineages are the same. Besides, they do not want to be in constant confrontation, affecting their livelihoods. They are also aware of the prevailing precarious living conditions in neighboring Islamic countries such as Pakistan and Afghanistan and the comfort and advancements in India.

In his very first Independence Day speech as the Prime Minister, Modi made an important statement that went unnoticed. "It's time all Indians come together as one, and work towards the progress of the nation and bring back the lost glory".

He meant it then and means it more now, having fulfilled the core agenda of the BJP for which it took birth.

>>>

**One cannot** forget a picture of Modi and Pope Francis fondly hugging each other.

Recently, during Christmas, Modi also hosted Delhi-based Christians of various sects at his home. He also met with Christian leaders in Kerala.

These reaching-out efforts are paying off, and it's evident in Kerala which has a high concentration of Christians. Several Christian leaders have joined the BJP.

Unlike between Hindus and Muslims where the discord is due to historical and religious reasons from the pre-independence era which is quite heavy, slight misgivings between Hindus and Christians is a post-independence development.

"Modi is not fit to be PM"

A lady head of a Christian-funded school, in Bengaluru, whom I have known for over a decade, said in utter disdain, in 2015.

"Modi was elected as PM a year ago. Why this comment now?", I asked her.

I knew that her school was managed by a Trust (NGO) and she was dependent on the foreign funds.

"Modi government is not releasing the funds of my Trust", she complained.

What she said is true.

Modi Government in one stroke, stopped thousands of crores of foreign funds that were coming into NGOs in India. It's also true that a huge chunk of these funds, though depicted as social service, were going into religious conversion.

Religious conversion was and is the only sore point between Christians and Hindus in India. This has been a serious social issue too.

Several Catholic friends of mine are against this "conversion ploy" adopted by various sects. Catholics themselves do not equate the recent converts with them.

Modi government did take severe steps to curb it.

That apart, there's nothing else between these communities. So, like in Goa or the Northeast, these communities bond well and come together for political benefits too. Kerala is next sooner or later.

>>>

**A B Vajpayee and** L K Advani were a famous formidable duo who built the BJP. The former was a dove and the latter, was a hawk. There arose another duo in the party later- Modi and Shah- both being hawks.

Vajpayee and Advani were equals. Vajpayee led the government and Advani the party - the BJP. There was a clear division of work and role clarity.

Nevertheless, Advani at times seemed to have some grouse against Vajpayee for always being his number two.

But Amit Shah doesn't. Shah seems very proud of Modi and happy to be his trusted lieutenant, follower, and *shishya.*

In every statement he makes, Shah chants "Modi".

Their rapport and trust that started in the 1990s brought them into the government when Modi became CM of

Gujarat. Shah was given multiple portfolios including Home by Modi, and was his clear No.2 in the Gujarat Government. But neither was he designated Deputy Chief Minister nor he aspired. He always remained Modi's Hanuman.

During the Sohrabuddin Sheikh fake encounter case, the Central agencies (Congress-led UPA was in power at the Centre) grilled Shah as he was the Home Minister of Gujarat and pressured him to turn against Modi but he didn't. Instead, as per the Court directive, he chose to leave Gujarat in 2010.

Shah follows Modi in toto. While leaving Gujarat for a year or so as per the Court directive, Modi sent Shah to Uttar Pradesh, the state that sends the highest number of MPs, with an instruction to study and connect with various social and political groups. It's this connection that helped Shah as the BJP's campaign-in-chief for UP in the 2014 Lok Sabha elections to micromanage and win 73 seats out of 80 for the party.

Shah is regarded as the Chanakya of BJP and Indian politics. But Modi is no less a Chanakya as he comes from the grassroots and has overcome multiple grinds. Modi himself is Chanakya+ Chandragupta but he has delegated "Chanakya's" role to Shah and ingrained in him such strategic abilities and has empowered him. Nevertheless, Shah is also rated very high on strategic thinking and organizational management.

This duo is the most powerful one in the Indian politics and governance. Notably, this duo is bonded by mission and merit rather than the "mutual convenience" that we see in most cases in politics.

Modi is a master of building a team and managing the team.

One thing with Modi is his uncompromising adherence to merit and delivery. He has an art of picking the right teammates. Once he develops confidence in them, he delegates and empowers them.

Nitin Gadkari has not always been on the best terms with Modi. Yet, he made him the Minister of Road Transport and Highways, the most vital area in Modi's mega infrastructure development plan. Because, Gadkari has consistently proven his ability in governance and execution, more so, in this specified area.

No one expected Nirmala Sitharaman to get pivotal Ministries such as Defence and Finance. Though she was a novice to the governmental administration, Modi entrusted her with these critical portfolios. Her character, commitment to ideology, and educational background (Economics) were the prime reasons.

External Affairs Minister Jaishankar is another example. During his first term as the Prime Minister, Modi was impressed with Jaishankar as US Ambassador and later, as the Foreign Secretary. After his retirement, he was made a Minister.

Ajit Doval, India's top-notch spymaster, has been the Modi Government's National Security Advisor since his first term.

Modi is very cautious and conscious of his teammates.

He accords importance to clean image, merit, and performance only. Political considerations do come but not for important portfolios.

Ex-Chief Minister of Karnataka Sadananda Gowda was given the railway ministry in the first term of Modi but he was shunted out almost immediately due to his non-performance. The same happened with Dr. Harshavardhan during COVID. Non-performers not only lose their ministries but political significance too.

During his firm term, Smriti Irani, one of the dependable and impressive women leaders of the BJP was made HR minister. But she went overboard at times. Besides, optics-wise, it was not going well with Modi's image. Her portfolio was changed and she was given a low-profile portfolio- Textiles. Nevertheless, she took on the prime leader of the opposition and the Congress Rahul Gandhi in Amethi again in 2019 and this time, defeated him in his family bastion.

Modi is also a master of shuffling teammates, both within the government and the party, and if needed, interchange. Rajnath Singh was the President of the BJP in 2013 when Modi was made the PM candidate. Rajnath Singh carries very clean credentials. By protocol, he is No.2 in the government peck. During the first term, Rajnath was Home Minister. But Modi had lined up very important things such as the abrogation of Article 370 during the second term. So, he brought in a more effective Shah to the Home Ministry and Rajnath was given the Defence Ministry. Still, Rajnath didn't raise any dissent or disgruntlement.

The biggest plus for Modi is that the BJP is a cadre and mission-driven party, and all its leaders are happy with the mission getting accomplished rather than personal aggrandizements. Besides, everyone knows Modi's selflessness, character credentials, commitment, hard work, and most importantly, vote-getting abilities. Hence, there's a total endorsement of his leadership by his team.

Another key skill Modi has is bringing the right people, and giving them the right place and at the right time. In 2014, Amit Shah could have taken into the Union cabinet. But, he was made the National President of the BJP. Modi knew the importance of building the party alongside the government and bringing in full synergy. Who could be better than Shah at that juncture?

He does empower his core teammates to make decisions but when they falter or the expected results are not delivered, he takes full charge, sets things right, and guides.

For example, during 2014-2019, Amit Shah was the President of the BJP. He was empowered to identify a suitable candidate for the Chief Ministership and appoint him. Appointing low-profile and cadre-based leaders as Chief Minister was a strategy as well as a directive. However, in a few states, the appointment of Chief Ministerial candidates mainly made by Amit Shah didn't yield the desired results, and Modi had to pitch in.

Modi also realized that only low-profile leaders will not be able to hold power in the states. The biggest and the most surprising decision made by Modi, after an emphatic victory in the 2017 Uttar Pradesh Assembly election, was to appoint a sulking, rebel leader Yogi

Adityanath as the Chief Minister. That proved to be a masterstroke and UP has been yielding more and more dividends to the party since then.

But the most astonishing of all about Modi is his total control of the team. In a nation rife with gossip, rumors, and information leaks, no whiff of major decisions such as the Balakot air strike, demonetization, or abrogation of Article 370 till they were done!

>>>

**Modi wants it all or none. For him, for his party, and for the nation.**

Vajpayee met with a shock defeat in 2004. Advani, the darling of the cadre but not so of the masses, as PM candidate lost in 2009.

Advani was the most towering leader of the party. On several occasions, I have personally seen Advani's "aura" and the respect he commanded from the leaders and the party workers as he built the party from scratch.

Advani again wanted to be the PM candidate in 2014. Despite Congress-led UPA's poor performance in the early 2010s, Dr Manmohan Singh as PM carried a good image. However, his age and physical inabilities were one sore point. Advani was also of the same age but he lagged behind Dr. Singh *vis-à-vis* image.

Even 2014 appeared to be a repeat of 2009. Most poll surveys indicated that. Still, Advani insisted on being the PM candidate. Modi objected.

After 2009, Modi started preparations silently for a national role. That's why, he had sent Shah to UP as early as 2010. He tapped into the situation, brought pressure on the BJP national leadership, and got nominated as PM candidate. Not a small thing to have "annoyed" the supreme leader Advani. But that's how Modi is! He is result-driven and he can bulldoze anyone within the party and the Opposition if someone comes in between.

After the 2014 victory, as per the modified BJP constitution of retiring anyone after 75 years from active politics, Advani had to retire and was made a member of Margdarshak Mandal (Guiding Body)

Nevertheless, his respect for Advani has not diminished to date. Notably, Advani and Vajpayee's images are still glaring at the very entrance of the national BJP headquarters in New Delhi. Advani has also been awarded recently with India's highest civilian honor- Bharata Ratna.

>>>

**Rahul Gandhi,** *de facto* boss of India's oldest party that originated in the pre-independence era, never assumed that he would ever see the challenge that Modi posed. If he had known Modi would make such an impact at the national level, probably, before Modi arose on the national horizon, he would have become the Prime Minister, at least from 2012 to 2014. Undoubtedly, Rahul shall have this regret for life as his chances of becoming the Prime Minister ever in his life appear slim.

During the same period as Modi arrived on the national scene in 2013, new hope and a fresh breeze in Indian politics had arrived in the form of the Aam Aadmi Party and its Chief Arvind Kejriwal.

While the Congress was already a national party and Rahul its supreme leader, Kejriwal planned to go all India at the very start. In his very first Lok Sabha elections. Kejriwal contested directly against Modi in Varanasi only to lose badly.

That was in 2014.

Now, it's 2024. Both Rahul and Kejriwal are on the decline, more so, at the national level.

Both of them who started as bitter rivals in 2014 have turned friends in 2024 to take on the juggernaut Modi.

Modi doesn't yield an inch to the competitors, rivals, and foes. He is ruthless. He goes after them non-stop. Modi virtually "strangulates" them.

It is with the Opposition and in politics, that Modi displays his "Chanakya *neeti*"- *sama* (conciliation), *dama* (gift/money/lure), *bheda* (division), and *danda* (punishment) - to the fullest. He knows when to deploy what of these four principles- together or separately.

Modi didn't have much of a challenge in 2019 as the Opposition was fully divided. But due to the changed circumstances by 2023, almost all the Opposition strived to come together under one banner INDIA (Indian National Developmental Inclusive Alliance).

Like Indira Gandhi in the 1970s, Modi occupied the center stage in Indian politics. All the Opposition parties united against Indira Gandhi in the 1977 Lok Sabha elections and succeeded in defeating her. In 2024, the same was intended by the Opposition parties to overthrow Modi.

Modi and the team worked overtime. He didn't want the psychological advantage to be with the Opposition which could have reduced the tally of the BJP and NDA though couldn't have been defeated.

*Sama, dama, bheda,* and *danda* were on full display.

The first to be targeted was Nitish Kumar, long-term Chief Minister of Bihar. Nitish has always been an open critic of Modi. He quit the National Democratic Alliance (NDA) in 2013 when Modi was anointed as the PM candidate. He joined hands with Congress and Rashtriya Janata Dal (RJD) in the 2015 Assembly elections and won an overwhelming majority. In 2017, he was back with the BJP and in the NDA. Just months before, the Central agencies had raided RJD's Lalu Prasad family in the "land for job" scam. Nitish always a stickler of clean image had a reason to rejoin NDA. Besides, he was also aware of the attempts being made by RJD to split JDU (Janata Dal-United) of Nitish. 2019 Lok Sabha elections, NDA swept Bihar.

NDA contested the Assembly elections together in 2020 and came to power. Nitish's JDU performed below par but was continued as CM. After a year, he again went back to RJD & Congress and formed the Mahagathbandhan government.

Nitish always nurtured Prime Ministerial ambitions. Being one of the senior leaders in the country and with a clean image, he thought he deserved it. So, in 2022 itself, he started mobilizing the Opposition forces to become united and take on the BJP/ Modi in the 2024 Lok Sabha elections. He almost succeeded in bringing most non-NDA parties together. Modi and the BJP watched every move closely. But Congress and RJD bungled. They didn't take Nitish into confidence. Once he realized he would not head the newly constituted Opposition's INDIA alliance, he was waiting for an opportunity to change sides.

Modi and co were working on the sidelines. All of a sudden, again, Nitish was given a reason. His and Bihar's socialist icon Karpoori Thakur was awarded Bharat Ratna, India's highest civilian honor. Nitish had a reason, was back in the BJP-led National Democratic Alliance(NDA) and they are fighting the Lok Sabha elections together in 2024.

Modi generally goes after his rivals full-on. But he also knows how to reach out. With Nitish, he has always followed the *Sama* (conciliation) principle as he knows if Nitish is on his side, Bihar is assured and his clean image is certified by another "clean leader".

It is "*Sama neeti*" Modi followed with Telugu Desam Party's Chandrababu Naidu too, recently, though Naidu had exited NDA in 2019 and traded diatribes against Modi. TDP is back in NDA for the 2024 Lok Sabha elections.

In Karnataka, Janata Dal Secular (JDS)'s HD Kumaraswamy in the 2018 Assembly elections, could have gone with the BJP and formed a coalition government. Instead, despite a lesser number of seats, for the Congress' offer of being made the Chief Minister, he went with them. Modi and the team waited for two long years. Congress' Siddaramaiah didn't like his *bete noire* H D Kumaraswamy heading the coalition government.

Some legislators of the Congress and also JDS resigned and supported the BJP Government headed by B. S. Yediyurappa. BJP was back in power in Karnataka.

If at all Modi respected any former Prime Minister, it was H D Deve Gowda, a non-Congress Prime Minister. But, Deve Gowda always flaunted "secular" credentials and opposed the "Hindu-centric" BJP. Still, Modi respected him. Now, for the 2024 Lok Sabha elections, JD-S has formally become a part of NDA. Again, Modi's *sama neeti.*

If someone goes against Modi and the BJP's hegemonic aspirations, it's *Bheda* (division/ dissension) and *Danda* (force/punishment). When he deploys these two *neetis* (principles) together, it's deadly. Not an iota of regret or sentiment in him even if they were once friends.

In Maharashtra, Uddhav Thackeray of the Shiv Sena had contested the 2019 Lok Sabha elections with BJP and they had swept Maharashtra. Subsequently, they swept the Assembly elections. Despite the BJP getting more seats, Uddhav Thackeray insisted on becoming Chief Minister, and he put forth the case of "Nitish as CM in Bihar" despite fewer seats. In the meantime, the ambitious satrap of Maharashtra BJP-Devendra Fadnavis along with Ajit Pawar of the Nationalist Congress Party (NCP) took oath as CM and Deputy CM in an overnight act. But that government fell flat as the NCP boss Sharad Pawar didn't budge.

Shiv Sena, NCP, and Congress came together and formed the government in Maharashtra.

Modi and co wait till the time is ripe and strike big. *Bheda* and *Danda* were in full force. Shiv Sena was split into two. NCP was split into two. Not just that, to ensure the BJP's image is not damaged, as a brilliant strategic move, Shiv Sena's splinter group leader Eknath Shinde was made the Chief Minister.

Shiv Sena boss Uddhav Thackeray and NCP's so-called Chanakya Sharad Pawar are sulking now.

If this could be the state of opposing regional satraps, no wonder Modi will wage a non-stop, full-throttle war against those eyeing his post, the Prime Minister of India. And those are Rahul Gandhi and Arvind Kejriwal.

When Modi is your opposition, you should never give him any room to attack you. But, Rahul Gandhi did. His biggest mistakes are three:

1. Born with "ascribed status" in the Congress's first family.
2. Despite having multiple opportunities to own responsibility and exhibit his abilities, he didn't.
3. Not rising to the challenge and level of Modi.

Having been born in the Congress' first family had given him many advantages- nationwide party base, over 25%

strong, ideologically committed vote share, etc. He could have capitalized on them.

But it was his missteps and wrongdoings that cost him dearly. From 2004 to 2014, while UPA was in power at the Centre, led by a reputed economist-cum-simpleton, Dr. Manmohan Singh, Rahul Gandhi could have been a part of the Ministry, learned so many things, delivered so many things, and made a name for himself.

Rahul came to be known as a man of power without responsibility. Besides, he used to get "invisible" suddenly and for a long period. He has corrected it of late and has been crisscrossing the country through *padayatra*s and many other sincere efforts such as the INDIA alliance. But it appears too little too late.

"*Shehzaada*" (prince) is the word Modi uses to address and attack Rahul Gandhi. And the way he uses is with utmost disdain and mockery.

Modi very carefully uses words. He has the art and craft of picking the right words and using them to the fullest effect.

*Shehzaada* is one such word. If at all Modi wanted to degrade Rahul's entitlement and call him a Prince, he could have used the Hindi word " Rajkumar". He instead chose the Urdu word *Shehzaada*. This reinforces the perception that Rahul Gandhi and the Congress are pro-Muslim and anti-Hindu.

Rahul did make a lot of efforts to shed his and his party's perceived anti-Hindu image. He offered prayers at multiple temples and declared he was a Shiv Bhakt.

But he declined the invitation to be a part of the Ayodhya Sri Ram Temple inauguration ceremony. What a blunder! What message did it send to the Hindu voters? Probably, he didn't want to alienate non-Hindu voters.

Rahul has been trying hard to take up issues to make a dent in Modi's image. He has achieved success at times.

One such verbal attack in the Parliament on Modi was Rahul's "suit-boot ki sarkar" which meant that the Modi Government sided with big business houses, particularly Adani. It did stick well and has become a point of discussion for long.

Wikipedia says- Adani Exports Limited started as a commodity trading company in 1988 and expanded into importing and exporting multiple commodities. With a capital of ₹5 lakhs, the company was established as a partnership firm with the flagship company Adani Enterprises, previously Adani Exports. In 1990, the Adani Group developed its port in Mundra to provide a base for its trading operations. It began construction at Mundra in 1995. In 1998, it became the top net foreign exchange earner for India Inc. The company began coal trading in 1999, followed by a joint venture in edible oil refining in 2000 with the formation of Adani Wilmar.

These timelines are very much before Modi became the Chief Minister of Gujarat. Adani was already into various businesses, and his focus since the beginning has been on infrastructure and logistics.

Gautam Adani hails from Gujarat, the same as Modi. When Gujarat and Modi were ravaged by the communal riots in 2002, and the official trade bodies revolted against Modi, it was Adani who stood by Modi and formed another trade body and also became an active part of the "Vibrant Gujarat" investment meets. Undoubtedly, there's a strong bond between both of them.

Modi is betting big on infrastructure development for India's progress and its manufacturing industry. Adani's core business is infrastructure and infrastructure management including port and airport management. There could be an alignment of thoughts but there's nothing to indicate there's nepotism in favor of Adani as many Opposition-ruled Governments at the state level have also awarded many projects to Adani.

But there were allegations that Adani eyed Mumbai airport and through the Modi government "arm-twisted" GVK Group to take it over from them. Rahul Gandhi raised this too, but GVK Group firmly denied it.

Adani Group has been rated very high globally for its efficient and cost-effective infrastructure development and management. It indeed rose to become the "most valued company" in India and made Adani one of the wealthiest persons in the world, overshadowing a fellow Indian and Asia's richest Mukesh Ambani. Then came the Hindenburg report, and the crash of Adani Group's market value only to gradually bounce back.

Nevertheless, Rahul Gandhi's continuous attack on Modi through the Adani Group has been in the news for long.

Rahul knew Modi's biggest strengths have been "his non-corrupt and tough leader" image. On the eve of the 2019 elections, Rahul's campaign slogan was "Chowkidar Chor Hain" (Watchman/ gatekeeper is a thief). Modi turned it to his advantage and declared, "Main hoon Chowkidar" (Yes, I am a watchman)

Rahul accused Modi of "cutting a deal" over the Rafale fighters' purchase and thus had compromised on the national security. It didn't have many takers, however.

Modi's strategies' impact and onslaught on Rahul Gandhi have been so severe that he lost from his home bastion Amethi in Uttar Pradesh in the 2019 Lok Sabha elections and won from the second seat, Wayanad in Kerala, far south.

On the eve of the 2014 Lok Sabha elections, Modi's "celibacy" and "brahmacharya" (bachelorhood) were attacked by accusing him of illegally snooping a woman. His educational qualification and caste status as OBC were questioned.

Congress leader Mani Shankar Aiyar called him a chaiwala (tea-seller). Modi countered, "Congress promotes only those born in "high families" and hates the poor and started a campaign "Chai pe *charcha*" (Discussion over tea)

Another Congress leader taunted Modi if he was from Harvard to manage the Indian economy. Modi thundered the next day at a rally, "*Mein* Harvard University *se nahin hoon. Mein* Hardwork University *se hoon.*" (I am not from Harvard University but from Hardwork University).

The Congress also tried to create a narrative- Modi instigated a communal riot to win the Gujarat Assembly elections in 2002. Modi also "planned" the Pulwama terrorist attack followed by the Balakot air strike to win the 2019 Lok Sabha elections.

The Opposition parties, particularly the Congress, have done everything possible not to spare Modi since he became the Chief Minister in 2001. He also went through a long trial in connection with the communal riots case. Nothing could be done.

Modi has been on the rise, and the Congress and Rahul Gandhi have been on the decline.

>>>

**In 2013-14,** another star originated in the Indian politics- Arvind Kejriwal.

The one who began his political career on a corruption eradication pitch in 2014, unfortunately, has landed up in a corruption scam in 2024.

An IIT graduate-turned-bureaucrat-turned-social activist, Kejriwal played an active role in Anna Hazare's Anti-Corruption Movement in 2011 which caught the attention of the nation. Corruption was at its peak then and the UPA Government at the Centre was caught in various scams.

While the Anti-Corruption Movement ended, much against the wishes of its leader Anna Hazare, and others, Kejriwal floated a political party Aam Aadmi Party.

Kejriwal did raise the people's hopes of a serious change in Indian politics. Those people who were opposed to conventional parties, Congress, and the BJP at the national level and fed up with caste-centric parties saw Kejriwal and AAP like a fresh breeze.

The people of Delhi did provide a chance to Kejriwal at his very first hustings, though not a full majority. Just to keep the BJP at bay, the Congress extended outside support to him and he formed the government. Despite becoming the Chief Minister, he was constantly in "agitations and protests" finally resigning from that position in early 2014 for not being able to table the Jan Lokpal Bill. Modi called him *"baghoda"* (the one who runs away)

Kejriwal plunged into the Lok Sabha elections instantly and contested against Narendra Modi in 2014 in Varanasi but lost badly. Modi came to power at the Centre. Nevertheless, in the Delhi Assembly elections that followed in a few months, AAP recorded a stupendous victory.

One of the first blunders Kejriwal committed was to alienate well-wishers and AAP's top leaders such as Prashanth Bhushan, Yogendra Yadav, Ashutosh, and Kumar Vishwas, who had helped him gain image and traction.

His constant confrontation with the Modi Government on one hand, and ambition to contest various state elections on the other hand, mostly in vain, did take a toll on him and his party.

In the 2019 Lok Sabha elections, despite Kejriwal having Delhi, lost all seven seats to the BJP. Nevertheless, he added one more state Punjab to his kitty where the BJP has been traditionally weak.

Modi was waiting to pounce. Kejriwal gave him an opportunity through the alleged liquor scam. Several ministers of the Delhi government are behind bars, and Kejriwal too.

Besides, Kejriwal whose battlecry was against Congress all these years has turned into its ally for the 2024 Lok Sabha elections. This could be the prime reason why Kejriwal has been targeted heavily.

What's in store for Kejriwal is hard to predict but his national and Prime Ministerial ambitions have dashed for now.

Modi is ruthless, Kejriwal often complained. Yes, he is.

>>>

**On the** eve of the 2019 elections, the Opposition had very strong issues such as demonetization and GST's botched-up implementation. But the Balakot air strike had neutralized everything and the tide had turned in Modi's favour. However, in a huge turnaround, currently, the same demonetization that led to the digital payment revolution and GST's record revenue collection are heralded as disruptive and revolutionary.

It should be noted that demonetization and GST implementation were opposed by most traders in Modi's home state Gujarat and had almost cost the BJP power in the Assembly elections that followed. But, Modi knew the long-term benefits of GST to the nation and formalizing the economy. So, for Modi, it is apparent that the national interests weighed more than the political interests. Another trait of Modi is, that he risks it all when the situation demands.

It's 2024. Modi is seeking a third consecutive term.

What are the key issues being raised by the Congress and allies against the Modi Government:

1.  Modi shall turn into an autocrat.
2.  India's democracy and Constitution are in danger.
3.  Modi is misusing/ abusing the Central Agencies to "finish off" the Opposition parties and leaders.
4.  Unemployment is on the rise.
5.  Inflation is out of control.
6.  Secularism is under threat.
7.  Caste census should be taken up across India, as backward castes, Scheduled Castes, and Scheduled Tribes have been ignored by the Modi Government.

Going by these issues that are being raised by the Opposition, it's a no-brainer to conclude that the Opposition is a non-starter in this election.

## 1.  Modi shall turn into an autocrat

Since my childhood, I have heard a lot of people say that India should have a "dictator" to streamline the country. By dictator, they meant a strong leader.

Modi has proven to be a strong leader through Covid management, the Balakot air strike, the abrogation of Article 370, etc.

Most people are not aware that Modi kept very few Ministries that too not so significant.

During his second term as Prime Minister, he had only the Ministry of Personnel, Public Grievances and Pensions, Department of Atomic Energy, and Department of Space.

Even as the Chief Minister of Gujarat, he had almost no ministry.

However, his PMO is very cohesive, well-orchestrated, well-managed, and well-controlled with an effective structure and efficient officers.

So is the case with his party BJP. They run it like a super MNC.

There have also been allegations of Modi curbing freedom of expression and the media. Being in the media industry, I have never heard any journalist saying that the Modi government stifling him or curbing his story unless it's "orchestrated, deliberate and against the national security". I know a few channels, more so, regional ones, who are 24x7 against Modi. They are very much operational. In Tamil Nadu, most channels are vociferous against Modi. They haven't been stopped despite the Ministry of Information & Broadcasting being with the Central Government.

In India, the sordid state of the television news channels is that most of them are funded by one or the political party and some are controlled by big corporate houses. And the Managements play stories according to their convenience rather than Modi "dictating" to them.

In the USA, Fox News is regarded as pro-Republicans and CNN as pro-Democrats. It's the respective Management's strategic decision to have content for their primary target groups or how a political following views a respective channel.

I have conducted several pieces of research about the viewership and have evolved strategies to boost the viewership. In one such research, an important insight that came out was that people wish to watch and watch longer, what their favorite people, celebrities, and *neta*s (political leaders) say and do. The people also prefer gluing to the news content they are attached to, ideologically. I am sure most news channels are also aware of these insights, and hence cater such leaders and stories to the biggest of their viewers. Currently, the largest of the viewers in India are nationalistic and rightist, which essentially means the BJP and Modi. That's why most channels are strategically vying for this "space" and hence, to some, it appears as if Modi has bought the media. It's strategic decisions made by the media companies to boost their viewership and revenues.

This has happened during my journalistic career too. During the 2004 Assembly elections in Karnataka while with ETV, an independent pre-poll survey was broadcast on our channel. It indicated that there would be a hung assembly and the BJP would be the single largest party, for the first time in Karnataka. A powerful Minister of the then Congress Government raised a hue and cry. The actual results that emerged were the same as our pre-poll prediction.

Exactly the opposite happened in the 2013 Karnataka Assembly elections. I had just resigned from my civil services position and had become CEO of a Kannada news channel. An independent survey there suggested that the Congress led by Siddaramaiah would emerge victorious. Then, the BJP people raised objections. What our independent survey had predicted turned true.

The current political scenario in India is such that all pre-poll surveys are indicating the third straight term for Modi. A popular English news channel calls it MOOD OF THE NATION. Modi is highly active on political as well as government fronts. Various programs of his are under constant gaze and draw appreciation from the general public. It is also true that the Modi government has been "scam-free".Naturally, most news houses cover these too. Though they all are facts, it appears that the media houses are biased, more so to the Opposition.

The news outlets do cover the Opposition too. But they are in a mess and have been continuously losing elections. This regular reportage of the Opposition appears biased even though they are very much the facts.

Recently, the Indian media elaborately covered a murky way of electing a BJP mayor in Chandigarh which was undone by the Supreme Court, and the AAP mayor was reinstated. Modi didn't meddle.

There are some independent and credible media houses in India and in terms of viewership and business, they are doing very well. The problem is with the politically funded news outlets, and that cannot be generalized.

Fake news on social media is a big issue worldwide. Many governments are bringing new regulations to curb it. Modi Government recently brought a notification establishing a Fact Check Unit (FCU) under the Press Information Bureau (PIB) to curb fake news against the Central Government. But the Supreme Court has stayed it immediately opining that it would curtail freedom of speech and expression.

The Supreme Court recently struck down the opaque electoral bonds scheme promulgated by the Modi government, stating that it leads to nexus and corruption and is dangerous to India's democracy.

One should note that the Indian Supreme Court is highly vigilant and shall act as true custodians of the Constitution and shall never allow anyone including Modi to become an "autocrat". The Indian public shall never accept it. Modi knows it too well and knows what happened to Indira Gandhi when she imposed "emergency". He shall continue to be a strongman but never an autocrat.

### 2. India's Democracy and Constitution are in danger.

Modi rose to dizzying heights only due to democracy. He has always been grateful to democratic principles and processes as a person of a humble origin like him got equal opportunity as others to contest, win, and become CM and PM. He may effect some changes to strengthen and smoothen democracy such as "One Nation One Election" but shall retain the vibrancy and basic structure of democracy as enshrined in the Indian Constitution. Besides, he has emerged as one of the global champions of free democracy.

All governments have effected amendments as the need and the situation demanded. Modi shall also bring in amendments to the Constitution as the situations and needs demand. Not more than that.

### 3. Modi is misusing/ abusing the Central Agencies to "finish off" the Opposition parties and leaders.

A string of leaders of the Opposition parties have been raided and arrested on various charges. The Central agencies are indeed on overdrive *vis-à-vis* several leaders of the Opposition parties. Even if so, these leaders could find justice if wrongly framed, in the courts of law. But in most cases, the charges have been proven right and have landed them in jail.

It has also been said that several Opposition leaders who were under the scanner of the Central agencies were pressured to join the BJP. There seems to be some truth in it.

Whoever was in the Opposition, always claimed "witchhunt" by the ruling dispensation through the central agencies.

The charges of misusing the Central agencies were leveled by Modi and Amit Shah too when they were put on a long trial for the Gujarat riots or Sohrabuddin fake encounter case.

Before the Supreme Court judgment on SR Bommai government VS Union of India in 1994, the Central government's agencies were not even known or required because if the Central leader didn't like any state leader or his government, the Centre directly dismissed the state government. The Congress Governments at the Centre at various junctures have dismissed many state governments- about 40 times.

A question that arises often in the current context is, why not any of the BJP leaders has been raided and whether all of them are clean. As one's experience in several BJP-ruled states including Karnataka goes, there have been several corrupt leaders but they have not come under the radar.

When someone is in power, using agencies and others for their convenience has always existed in India and the most democratic countries. But it is no justification if Modi if at all is using the Central agencies selectively and indiscriminately.

It's the Opposition that always needs to be cautious in every deed particularly when they are up against "ruthless Modi" and " master of Chanakya *neeti*". With one slip, they are down the slope forever.

### 4.  Unemployment is on the rise.

Highly disruptive demonetization in 2016 and the devastating COVID have had a serious impact on the economy and jobs. Nevertheless, while the world is still recovering, the Indian economy has already shown resilience and has been consistently the fastest-growing large economy. It's no more in "Fragile Five" like in 2013. Stock markets are on a constant rise.

During this period, India has also become the world's most populated nation, with 144 crores. Crores of the youth are coming into the job market every year.

According to the Forbes India website, the unemployment rate during 2010-13, pre-Modi, was around 5.5% and the same level continued till 2019. During COVID years, it had gone up to 8%. In early 2024, it was at 6.57%.

So, except for the COVID years, the unemployment rate has been the same during pre-Modi and post-Modi years.

Modi government has given a lot of emphasis to skill development programs. But they are more for blue-collar jobs suitable to the manufacturing sector. Skill courses that boost white-collar jobs need to be accorded equal importance.

When China faced a massive unemployment problem in the 1970s, the solution they found was to build massive infrastructure and boost the manufacturing sector. That's what Modi's endeavor also has been.

However, post-demonetization, the MSME sector, the highest employment provider, has been affected. Modi government has come out with various schemes to strengthen this sector but some more concerted effort is essential.

Start-ups are increasing day by day across India including tier-2 cities which is a good sign. Undoubtedly, the Modi government has been striving to build an effective start-up ecosystem. The most critical components to fuel start-ups are timely, essential funds and "initial stage guidance". In the interim budget of 2024, the government has allocated Rs.22,000 crores but efficient disbursement has to be ensured. Apt economics methodologies are also to be employed in assessing, allocating, and disbursing necessary funds to the start-ups and MSMEs. The approach has to be flexible.

There have also been cases of mediators at the ground level who discriminate and demand favors to get the loans disbursed. More transparency and direct disbursements should be ensured.

### 5. Inflation is out of control.

A leading global website focus-economics.com writes: "India witnessed moderately high inflation from 2013 to 2022, generally oscillating between 4% and 6%. Over the past decade until 2022, consumer price inflation in India averaged 5.5%, In January 2024, it eased to 5.10%."

However, just to juxtapose with Dr. Manmohan Singh-led UPA Government-II, the inflation rate in 2010 was 12%, and in 2013, 10.9%, twice that of the Modi dispensation.

The Opposition doesn't have a strong argument to attack the Modi government on this.

The average inflation target set by RBI in consultation with the Government is 4%.

### 6. Secularism is under threat.

Rahul Gandhi talks often about his "idea of India" which means "secular India" where all religions are equal and exist in total harmony, and complains that Modi is endangering the "secular fabric" of India which will result in societal and religious disharmony.

Modi doesn't hide either. His ideology is that of RSS and BJP- the primary place is accorded to Hinduism in the land of its birth and his every deed reflects it.

Primacy, however, doesn't mean subjugating others.

Rahul Gandhi carries the pre-independence Congress ideology employed by India's first Prime Minister Jawaharlal Nehru of "inclusiveness" though it is considered appeasement by his opponents. Modi carries pre-independence born- Rashtriya Swayam Sevak's (RSS) core philosophy of "Hindus form the core and the center of India (Hindustan)".

The Indian National Congress was formed in 1885. RSS was born in 1925.

While the Congress has been a political organization, RSS is fundamentally a "volunteer organization"/ social organization ingrained with the core philosophy of " the Hindus first".

The Congress gained power "automatically" post-independence. RSS formed its political wing Akhila Bharatiya Jana Sangh (ABJS) in 1951 which was rechristened as "Bharatiya Janata Party" (BJP) in 1980, and strived incessantly to topple the Congress and gain power.

Jana Sangh lost one of its Founders Shyama Prasada Mukherjee during an agitation in Kashmir against Article 370 in 1953. Mukherjee was arrested and jailed by the Nehru Government. He developed some complications and died while in custody which raised suspicions. There was pressure on Nehru to form an independent inquiry commission to probe his death but he didn't.

The Congress and the BJP have contrasting ideologies and have always been at loggerheads. The partition of India based on religious lines was the first serious flashpoint. The RSS' role was alleged in the assassination of Mahatma Gandhi in 1948. The

Congress Government banned RSS then and a few other occasions.

The RSS strived for decades to gain power at the Centre to reassert Hinduism. It found the first phase of success in the 1990s post-Ram Janma Bhoomi movement. It is seeing its best phase currently in the form of Modi.

Modi is a child of RSS as he was introduced and inducted into it when he was just eight years old. He has ingrained both ideological and cultural moorings of RSS. Like most RSS men, he is virtually a bachelor (Though he was married under his parents' compulsion, he left home the same night). He has emerged as the real poster boy of RSS. He has already fulfilled the core agenda of the BJP-Abrogation of Article 370, Ayodhya Sri Ram temple, and Uniform Civil Code ( being implemented in the BJP-ruled states one by one).

BJP and its coalition NDA's first Prime Minister Atal Behari Vajpayee was moderate and was quite hesitant to exhibit RSS and BJP's core credentials, probably due to the coalition compulsions. That is considered the reason why he lost RSS and BJP cadre faith and lost the 2004 Lok Sabha elections which were tipped in his favor.

Modi has no hesitation at all. After winning from Varanasi and becoming the Prime Minister in 2014, he offered prayers and aarti amid shlokas on the banks of the river Ganga at Kashi Viswanath Dham. It was the first of its kind sight in Indian politics. The Hindus felt at home for the first time. That's it. That was the beginning of the resurgence and mainstreaming of Hinduism in its motherland, not just in independent India but in over 1000 years.

While flaunting other religious symbols by the Hindu leaders was the norm in politics till then, since the advent of Modi, Hindu leaders of other parties have been compelled to "showcase" their Hindu heritage and credentials. Rahul Gandhi is no exception.

There has always been a confrontation between "Bhartiya" religions such as Hinduism, Sikhism, Jainism, Buddhism, and the foreign, Abrahamic religions such as Islam and Christianity.

Generally, the BJP leaders' key thoughts are as follows: "The implementation of Uniform Civil Code was enshrined in the Indian Constitution under the Directive Principles. Nehru could have easily implemented it, and it would have made all citizens one and equal. That would have also assuaged the Hindus who were deeply aggrieved by the division of Bharat. Instead, like the pre-independence era, Hindus were ignored, the Muslims were pampered and the Christians were encouraged. The Hindu population kept dwindling and the Muslim and the Christian population kept increasing"

What is Secularism? Secularism is an ideology that says religion should not be involved with the ordinary social and political activities of a country. It dictates that there is no official religion of the state.

Yes, most democratic countries including India do not have an "official state religion". Yet, the political systems have "not been devoid of religions".

A community's core culture originates through its religion. Most cultural representations are also linked to their religion in one way or the other.

Politics is nothing but marketing and applying marketing logic, principles, and strategies at every step. Like any "brand", a political party is also a brand. Any good brand shall devise its "core philosophy/vision/mission" too. It has its own primary, secondary, and tertiary target groups.

The Congress claims to be "secular" and "all-inclusive". It's the voters who decide. The Congress is on the downside means, it must be short of appealing to the most. Or as the BJP accuses, most voters could be considering Congress as a "pseudo-secular" and "minority appeaser" and could be rejecting it.

The Congress accuses the BJP of majoritarianism at the cost of the minorities. It has been conveniently considered and projected that Muslims, with over 20 crore population, and Christians, with over four crore, as minorities. Then, what about Jews who are below 5,000 and Parsis with just 70,000 people? Do these "miniscule minorities" raise the same complaint that Secularism is under threat in India? Because they know India intrinsically accommodates all and accords equal respect and status to all.

Yet, both parties are right. Both talk to their " target religious groups".

And, which democratic country in the world doesn't target communities based on social, cultural, and religious moorings and preferences, at least subtly?

In Pakistan, Islam is at the center of politics. In the US, puritanism and non-puritanism based on Christianity are often considered in the voters' preferences, and thus, the political parties and leaders position accordingly. Hinduism has taken center stage in Indian politics, and it's going to stick and stay.

"The Hindu Nationalist" Bharatiya Janata Party (BJP)- This is how the Western media introduces or addresses the party in all its news articles. Modi doesn't mind. His party has positioned that way, and its supreme leader, Modi embodies it and enlivens it.

**7. Caste census should be conducted across India, as backward castes and Scheduled Castes and Scheduled Tribes have been ignored by the Modi Government.**

During the recent Assembly elections in late 2023, Rahul and the Congress leveled allegations that the BJP and Modi are not giving due place to OBCs, the largest social group in India, and are also not making OBCs the Chief Ministers in the BJP-ruled states. The Congress fared miserably as against its stellar performance in the last Assembly elections in those states five years ago.

This charge doesn't stick with OBCs as the biggest-ever leader from that social block is Modi. Modi doesn't like invoking caste, still, he did occasionally emphasize that he was from a poor and backward caste.

The Congress and the other Opposition parties also alleged that Modi got his caste included in the OBC list in Gujarat after he became the Chief Minister. However, the truth is that his caste Modh-Ghanchi was included in Gujarat by a Congress Government in the 1990s.

The Scheduled Castes (SC) and Scheduled Tribes (ST) connect more with OBCs. There's no discrimination in any of the government schemes. Besides, Ramnath Kovind, the previous President nominated by the Modi government belongs to SC, and the current President Draupadi Murmu is from the ST community.

What are the key issues, planks, and narratives raised by the Opposition that would gain traction against Modi in the 2024 Lok Sabha elections?

As said before, the Opposition had the best of the issues against Modi in 2019 such as demonetization and GST. So, it appears that " Secularism is under threat, the Constitution is under threat, Central agencies are being misused to trample the Opposition, and Modi would turn into an autocrat" against Modi may not yield dividends as they have been used earlier, and are not directly affecting the common voters.

It's also interesting that the Opposition has not raised anything related to COVID-19 management including the suddenly imposed nationwide lockdown. During the second term, Modi's biggest achievement has been the COVID situation management.

Apart from attacking Modi, what's that the Congress is pitching? It's 'five nyay' (justices) — 'Bhagidari Nyay'

(Participatory), 'Kisan Nyay' (Farmers), 'Nari Nyay' (Women), 'Shramik Nyay' (Workers), and 'Yuva Nyay' (Youth) — giving 25 guarantees, five under each category,

It's refreshing to see that Congress has not used social groups such as castes and religions in its manifesto. Instead, it has used economic groups. It's also interesting to note that Hindi words have been used to describe them, and not English like in earlier years.

Interestingly, both these- strategizing on " these four core economic groups" and primacy to Hindi- have been the effect of Modi on the Opposition and in Indian politics.

In contrast to the Opposition, Modi's key pitches to the voters in the 2024 Lok Sabha elections are:

-   Viksit Bharat (Developed India) by 2047
-   The world's third-largest economy during his third term.
-   Emphasis on the infrastructure that would be on par with the US.
-   Boosting the manufacturing sector that would result in massive employment opportunities.
-   Importance to tech sectors such as AI, semiconductors, and space.
-   Better health infrastructure, *pucca* houses for the poor, and several others that better "ease of living".
-   Reducing corruption

All the above are packaged, pitched, and promoted under the slogan- "Modi ki guarantee"

**Modi ki** guarantee!?

In the most recent Assembly elections, guarantee had become a buzzword. Offering a wide range of freebies, the Congress in Karnataka devised a superb campaign under the duo of Siddaramaiah and D.K. Shivakumar titled "Karnataka Congress ki guarantee". The Congress defeated the ruling BJP.

In Telangana, another major state in the south, the Congress ran a similar campaign- Telangana Congress ki guarantee with a range of freebies. The Congress trounced the ruling Bharat Rashtra Samiti (BRS).

Modi is very quick to learn and pick. Before Congress could use "guarantee" for the national elections, Modi "usurped" this buzzword and coined "Modi ki guarantee".

In the backdrop of the Balakot air strike, on the eve of the 2019 LS elections, a solid campaign line was coined- "Modi *hai toh mumkin hai*" (With Modi, everything is possible). It was a hit and the voters admitted that.

The "Modi ki guarantee" campaign theme for the 2024 elections is already a hit among the voters. The voters are not complaining about it or mocking it. All seem to believe in his guarantee, except the Congress and the Opposition and their hard-core followers.

The results seem to be a foregone conclusion, firmly in favor of the BJP and NDA. The only question is whether another slogan of Modi " Is baar 400 paar" (This time, over 400 seats" is going to become a reality.

A quick SWOT analysis of BJP/NDA and Congress/INDI Alliance will ascertain this.

| | | BJP/NDA VS CONG/INDI ALLIANCE | | | |
|---|---|---|---|---|---|
| SL NO | ATTRIBUTE/S | BJP/NDA description | BJP/ NDA 0-10 SCORE | CONG/ INDIA description | CONG/ INDIA 0-10 SCORE |
| 1 | PM Candidate | Modi's governance credentials | 10 | Rahul Gandhi's governance credentials | 0 |
| 2 | PM Candidate's skillset | Modi's hard work, oratory skills, decisiveness, discipline, etc | 10 | Rahul Gandhi's hard work, oratory skills, discipline, etc | 3 |
| 3 | PM Candidate's persona | Modi's charisma, charm, and vote-pulling abilities | 10 | Rahul Gandhi's persona, charm, and vote-pulling abilities | 3 |
| 4 | Top Team | Shah, Nadda, efficient state chieftains etc | 8 | Not so well-known Cong's Top Team, state chieftains, etc | 5 |
| 5 | Research, Planning, Strategy & Execution | Very well-oiled, constant war mode machinery | 10 | Haphazard, last-minute efforts | 3 |

| SL NO | ATTRIBUTE/S | BJP/NDA description | BJP/ NDA 0-10 SCORE | CONG/ INDIA description | CONG/ INDIA 0-10 SCORE |
|---|---|---|---|---|---|
| 6 | Workers/ Cadre | Well-directed, ideologically-determined, totally inspired and confident | 10 | Reasonably strong and ideologically driven, Left to local chieftains, no clear direction | 4 |
| 7 | Booth Management | Managing the voters, convincing them, and bringing them to the booths to vote is exemplary | 10 | Congress except in a few states is glaringly weak | 4 |
| 8 | Issues/ Narratives | Proven governance, Putting India on the global arena, Viksit Bharat, developed economy by 2047, corruption-free, poverty-free Bharat, Unity, Strong leadership, weak, corrupt, dynastic Opposition etc | 10 | Attacking Modi as being an autocrat, secularism is in danger, etc and failing to project an alternative vision to the country. | 3 |
| 9 | Financial Resources | The world's largest political party is also well-funded | 10 | Depleted | 2 |
| 10 | Coalition | Strong in most states and weak in a few states | 6 | Strong in a few states and very weak in most states | 4 |

| SL NO | ATTRIBUTE/S | BJP/NDA description | BJP/NDA 0-10 SCORE | CONG/ INDIA description | CONG/ INDIA 0-10 SCORE |
|---|---|---|---|---|---|
| 11 | Voters' groups | "Primary target group" of Hindu & development-driven neutral secondary group | 7 | The primary target group of minorities and possibly, some: marginalized sections | 4 |
| 12 | Government schemes' beneficiaries | Modi government and various BJP state governments' programs have created a massive number of beneficiaries | 10 | Congress has not been in power at the Centre for 10 years and very few governments at the state, so fewer beneficiaries | 3 |
| 13 | Indian diaspora influence and support | Modi Government has been of great help and support to the Indians abroad and has also airlifted the needy several times; Modi's addresses to the diaspora whenever he is on foreign tours. | 10 | Ideologically attached supporters only | 3 |

| SL NO | ATTRIBUTE/S | BJP/NDA description | BJP/ NDA 0-10 SCORE | CONG/ INDIA description | CONG/ INDIA 0-10 SCORE |
|---|---|---|---|---|---|
| 14 | Historical baggage | BJP is a relatively new party and Modi is its second PM. And they have not committed any historical blunders to be attacked | 0 | Congress has a long history and the BJP has been constantly hammering on their past "failures" and "blunders" | -6 |
| | TOTAL MARKS | | 121/140 | | 35/140 |

>>>

**What makes** Modi such a phenomenon?

What makes him a non-stop winning machine?

What makes him the darling of the masses?

What makes him "the *mahaan* in the making?"

Just one-line answer- It's the organization- The Rashtriya Swayamsevak Sangh (RSS)- he was born in and the organization- the Bharatiya Janata Party (BJP)- that he is further building and through both of them, the nation India that he is building.

>>>

**Only when** one attempts to build an organization, he will realize the importance of the organizations already built and the people behind them.

I am in the process of building such an organization. After going through many unforeseen circumstances, constraints, and challenges, I sincerely admire the Organization I was born in and its Founder.

Building the world's largest film city in the parched lands is not a joke. That's Ramoji Film City on the outskirts of Hyderabad.

Building India's largest television brand and the most deeply penetrating news network is nothing short of a miracle. That's India's first pan-India television brand ETV and its Founder, India's original media tycoon Sri Ramoji Raogaru. This is the Organization I was born in, and whatever organization (VISHVAGRA) I am endeavoring to build, is on those lines.

Another organization that took birth after my birth and has grown to dizzying heights is of great interest ( as a journalist, I don't say "influence") to me is the Bharatiya Janata Party.

>>>

For any Organization to succeed and become great, my formula of 7Ms will have to be in place and sync:

1. Mission
2. Mentor
3. Master
4. Men
5. Money
6. Machine
7. Management

From my four years of directly working under Sri Ramoji Rao Garu, the Honorable Chairman of Eenadu Group, and innumerable interactions and instructions I have had with him, this is what I could deduce out of the organization and its frontal brand ETV.

BRAND: ETV

1.  Mission- Building pan India regional television news network that "gathers news" directly in the field, and offers an authentic and whole range of news to its viewers, presented in a neat, lucid manner.

2.  Mentor- Honourable Chairman Sri Ramoji Rao himself.

3.  Master- Sri Ramoji Rao himself.

4.  Men (Key)- S Ramanujan as News Director (during my initial days), Bapineedu as the Operations Director, Gopal Rao as HR Director, Subba Naidu as the Operations Head of Bengaluru/Karnataka, etc. They all were together with Sri Ramoji Raogaru for several decades and had built this mammoth organization brick by brick. He also selected the right chieftains who could take forward the organizational philosophy and strategies.

5.  Money: "Manju, running a business is not easy. Beg, borrow, or steal, I have to mobilize money on time to keep things running", I remember him saying. I couldn't understand its depth then, as a 30-year-old *baccha* (kid) as he used to fondly call me.

Sri Ramoji Raogaru is a strict stickler of time- his meetings or LIVE news. Not late by a second. Our LIVE prime bulletin should start at 9 PM sharp on all 12 channels, every night.

Once, we got an instruction from Operations that our LIVE prime news bulletin would start at 9.03 PM for a few days, and at 9 PM, there would be LIVE lottery results called PLAYWIN ( That's the name I remember). We the news chieftains were shocked in utter disbelief. Being his *shishya* (disciple), later I asked my Chairman politely about it. He just said, " I understand". We came to know later that the organization had a financial crunch, and PLAYWIN lottery had offered a premium for this.

While building my organization VISHVAGRA, I have realized that money is not just fuel but also the engine. And if money doesn't come in on time, the organization can collapse and the team can crumble. That's what happened to me, my team of over 60 members, and my company recently when an investor who had come on the Board of the company didn't make the committed investment. One of the purposes of writing this book, my very first book, in great urgency is to get some money through book sales, resurrect the careers of my teammates, and rebuild the company.

ETV never delayed the salary of its thousands of employees across India or payments to its vendors. Having taken a major beating due to the investment not happening as committed by the investor and my team going through a really tough time, I love ETV's Honorable Chairman, much more now for all the pain he took, the financial planning he made, and the financial commitments he honored.

6.  Machine: ETV had floors and floors of huge studios with state-of-the-art infrastructure at all levels, national, state, and district levels, and earth station. It was one of the main reasons for the smooth and hassle-free operations of such a massive network.

7.  Management: Till I was with ETV, the Honorable Chairman was at the helm of management, and all operations were efficiently handled by his core team of men. The news was always treated with the highest sanctity. I have strategized and coordinated several all-India news events including the 2004 Lok Sabha elections, during my days with ETV. Not a single time did I get any instruction to change a news item or oppose or favor anyone. ( Though there were murmurs that in the Telugu channel, TDP was favored a bit, yet as I was never a part of the Telugu channel, I knew nothing of that sort)
To date, the brand ETV, which currently runs the ETV Bharat news app in all languages and covers all states, which I rate as the best in India, has stood steadfast for news integrity and sanctity.

>>>

**The other** Organization that has fascinated me for its phenomenal growth is the BJP, Is being described based on my 7M principles::

BRAND: The Bharatiya Janata Party (BJP)

1. Mission- Building Hindu-centric, holistically developed Bharat and making it Vishwaguru.

2. Mentor- RSS/ Sarsanghchalak (currently)- Dr. Mohan Madhukar Rao Bhagwat(currently)

   99 years ago, when India was still under British rule, Rashtriya Swayamsevak Sangh (RSS) was started by K.B.Hedgewar. This has become the world's largest volunteer organization and its political wing BJP has become the world's largest political party, and is at the helm of Bharat with its core ideology being implemented.

   It's a wonderful case study to study the vision of the RSS Founder and the way he nurtured his first team, who then kept building team after team and sustained the same ideology and spirit despite so many obstacles. Amazing!

3. Master (currently)- Narendrabhai Damodardas Modi

   The "master" that RSS, BJP, and affiliates strived to build for decades has finally manifested in the form of Modi. As Modi firmly believes in the core ideology of the organizations he was bred in and follows them in toto, these organizations too believe in Modi and back him in toto.

4. Men (Key)- Currently, in the BJP, Amit Shah, J. P. Nadda, and B. L. Santosh are key drivers. Ideology-

ingrained cadre is its biggest strength and they man all key posts at all levels.

5. Money- The Opposition alleges that the BJP is very well-funded today. Not surprising. It's the largest political party in the world and thus, voluntary contributions from its members are one source. It has a government at the Centre and in various states. So, corporates do contribute/ donate to this party as well as other parties of their choice. It also has a very good financial management/treasury system.

   It was not so however till a decade ago. Lakhs of the RSS and BJP workers used to have half a meal a day and sleep in railway stations. Besides, RSS and BJP have built on austerity and simplicity.

   It also deserves a study to understand how the RSS and BJP managed to sustain and build the organizations that they are today, without financial resources for over eight decades.

6. Machine- The BJP has the best management ground/booth network, political management infrastructure, research wing, MIS, IT cell, promotion wing, war room, etc. It operates in such a seamless manner that even the biggest of the MNCs should ape it.

7. Management- It has a very well-planned Organizational structure and hierarchy headed by the National President and operations helmed by the Organizing Secretary. Their strategic management

and deployment and their continuous war mode are their biggest strength. There's a tight grip over several crores of their karyakartas as well as several thousands of elected leaders. A small act of misconduct invites immediate disciplinary action.

In the 2024 Lok Sabha elections, rabble-rousing and "hate-spilling" MPs were denied the tickets.

>>>

**What catapulted** Modi to this soaring height is the combination of RSS culture and his unique traits and several factors adding to one another:

Factor 1: Hindu, Hindustan & Hindi.

RSS is the mother, father, the first family, *guru,* and *gurushala* of Modi.

RSS's vision, as well as the mission, is to "Have immense pride in the Hindu heritage and culture; Hindus form the core of Hindustan, and Hindi should become the primary language that connects all Hindus".

It's usually alleged that RSS nurtures mostly Brahmins and other castes are not given equal opportunity. Modi is a classic example of busting that.

It has strictures for its *swayamsevaks* and *pracharaks* in terms of culture, attitude, knowledge, and etiquette that include bachelorhood, austerity, simplicity, non-alcoholism, and vegetarianism. "Hinduism, the oldest surviving religion, has a rich heritage and was vast as

"Akhand Bharat" (Undivided India) and its glory has to be re-established" is the core philosophy that's ingrained in.

RSS turns 100 next year (2025) and what a way to celebrate its moment of triumph and fulfillment of its major mission in the form of its poster boy Narendra Modi, being at the helm of Bharat and through Modi- the full embodiment of RSS!

Modi has also fulfilled the core agenda of the BJP, the political wing of RSS, considered impossible till it was done- abrogation of Article 370 and "rejoining" Kashmir- the "head" of Bharat with its body, and inauguration of grand Sri Ram Mandir at Ayodhya.

Their next joint mission is to make Bharat, Vishwaguru (The world's teacher/leader).

Hence, the campaign of Viksit Bharat (Developed India) has begun and shall go on till 2047. For that, Modi and other set of leaders like Modi are required for the next three decades.

To accomplish its next milestone, Sangh Parivar as RSS and its affiliates are called, henceforth doesn't have many challenges that it had hitherto. Complacency and overconfidence should not set in, though.

Factor 2: Changing the Indian voters

The whole of India was Congress in the 1970s and early 80s when Indira Gandhi was at its helm. "India was Indira; Indira was India". With regards to "worshipping" Indira, my family was no different from the rest of India.

In a small town Krishnarajanagar near Mysore, without any TV or social media, Indira was still ruling the hearts of most Indians. My father was no different.

As my father was a municipal councilor, while I was a kid, I was exposed to basic political activities such as pamphlets, parties, leaders, campaigns, etc.

In our small town, another political party that had gained a foothold was the Janata Party, born a decade ago, to oppose the Indira-imposed emergency.

 It was the first time, in 1985-86, when I was entering an undergraduate course, I heard of another party-Bharatiya Janata Party (BJP).

I was very active in sports and extracurricular activities, at the college and in my *mohalla*. A middle-aged person used to come to our cricket ground and talk to us casually. We came to know each other quite well. Now and then, he took us to his nearby home, offered tea and biscuits, and got into general conversation with us. TV was a rarity those days, but he was privileged to have a color TV, and we used to watch sports once in a while.

One fine day, he took us all to his home. He appeared very emotional and agitated. He played a video with a VCR. It was a documentary on the prevailing insurgency in Jammu & Kashmir and atrocities on the Hindus.

We knew him as a nice gentleman working for LIC. Only later, we came to know that during his free time, he propagated the RSS mission as a *pracharak*( preacher). He was married though.

For a small-town guy, RSS, *Pracharak*, etc were new words.

By this example, what I meant is the RSS was so deep within the society, and how hard it worked on the ground laying the edifice to the BJP.

Then I stepped into Manasa Gangotri, the Mysore University campus, to study M.Sc. It was then I heard of Akhila Bharatiya Vidyarthi Parishad. Those students, though small in number, were constantly raising the Kashmir issue. That's where I heard for the first time about Article 370.

Those were the days of Rajiv Gandhi as the Prime Minister, getting replaced by his one-time confidante V P Singh, the Mandal movement by Janata Dal, and Sri Rama Janmabhoomi movement by the BJP. India was on a churn.

>>>

**In the** initial years of the BJP, the RSS culture percolated among the BJP workers (*karyakartas*) too. Their simple and austere lifestyle and nationalistic pitch started appealing to the voters.

In my small town Krishnarajanagar, I have experienced two things about building something from scratch:

There was not a single Christian-led, English-medium convent in my small town in the 1970s. St. Joseph's Convent was new and their culture and offerings were fresh. Nuns, called sisters, in light blue gowns, visited house to house, and spread the message of "English and its importance in carving the future of their sons and daughters". They did make a lot of effort. My elder sister was in one of the initial batches, and I followed after four years. To be honest, quality education was their only mission. We had not even heard of Christianity or heard of Christ. There were some images of Christ and the "sisters" followed their customs but not once, there was any attempt at any Christian teachings. However, every year, they used to take us to St.Anthony's Church at nearby Doranahalli, terming it as a picnic. Still, it made me curious to know about Christ. I loved Christ's persona, suffering, sacrifice, and message to mankind, and have also offered prayers at some Churches.

After some years, the same St.Joseph's Convent saw long lines of applicants and now is the largest and the most sought-after educational institution in my hometown.

Another such institution/ organization is the BJP.

The way the nuns and sisters of the Convent went door-to-door with a simple dress code and beneficial message, the BJP *karyakartas*- simple-looking and nation-driven, came as fresh political ambassadors. They subsisting on plain water and bananas were also talk of the town.

In every town, there were only one or two leaders (as coordinators who emerged as leaders), *karyakarta*s were a few and the voters were nil.

This must have been the situation across the country for the BJP in the 1980s. See where it is now- all-pervasive and the most dominant political force in this vast, the world's most populated country and the world's largest democracy.

That's why, the BJP's top leadership including Modi who started as *karyakarta*s extols its current *karyakarta*s and accommodates them in the party and the government's top echelon.

>>>

**Due to** such concerted efforts by the RSS and the BJP in the 80s, the Congress I was introduced to and inducted into by my father was slowly ceding space to the Janata Dal and Bharatiya Janata Party. In the forthcoming years, Janata Dal got divided into several splinter groups across the country as they lacked ideological bonding unlike the BJP which stood in unison and kept growing and expanding "as a party with a difference".

RSS, ABVP, and BJP were successfully "changing the voters" and building the voters, notably, with strong ideological moorings.

Factor 3: Voters were changing.

There was no Indira in the Congress or Indira-like leader in any other party. A streak of coalition governments and weak leaders was harming the interest and image of India.

Advani had firmly emerged as the toughest and Vajpayee as the best among all leaders from across the political spectrum. Even the neutral voters were taking note.

Advani and the BJP had reignited the resurgent feeling among the Hindus. Besides, another set of voters was seeking a stable government with strong leadership, which could take India and their lives to the next level.

BJP was given a chance at the Centre under Vajpayee and performed well too. However the core Hindu voters were not happy as he didn't endeavor to take up the party's core issues and didn't take an active part in the 2004 hustings, and the BJP lost. It is to the credit of Sonia Gandhi that she regrouped the Congress and its allies and presented a formidable coalition that ruled for 10 years.

Factor 4: Increased unrest and aspirations among the voters.

Scams of the UPA-2 government along with uncontrolled inflation and other factors had caused severe unrest among the masses. Getting better connected with the world through TV and internet, the youth were getting more aspirational. The average Indian voter wanted someone who would be scam-free, strong, and development-driven. Modi emerged on the scene and won a massive mandate in 2014, getting an absolute majority after 30 years.

Factor 5: Exposing the facts/truths "hidden" by the Congress.

The BJP had deployed another ammunition- exposing the Congress's past lies and hidden truths. This intensified after 2013 when Modi and social media took center stage.

Have you ever heard of the Indian Naval Mutiny in 1946? Do you know that it was one of the reasons that compelled the British to give up India in a hurry?

I appeared for the Karnataka Civil Services exam in 1998. I qualified too. For that, I must have studied Indian history and polity extensively, right?

We had a separate paper on the Indian National Movement. But, there was not a single word on the Indian Naval Mutiny of 1946.

I came to know about it only after 2014, that too, through social media.

I also recalled what I studied in Social Studies in High School, and various papers given for the Civil Services Exams. Post High School, I had chosen the Science stream and was not exposed to humanities subjects such as Sociology, Political Science, History, etc

For the Civil Services Exam, I chose Sociology and History as my main subjects. Under Sociology, more space was given to the pitfalls of Hinduism, the caste system, and its evils, and not much on how the Indian/Hindu society evolved from 10,000 BC, how Hinduism was different, and how it survived the onslaught of various religions.

The chapters under the Indian History didn't give much importance to pre-10th Century AD where it was ruled by the Hindu kingdoms and their accomplishments. The most elaborate sections were "The Great Mughals" and then, how the British and English "added value" to India.

In the Indian Polity post-independence, we never read anything about Nehru passing on the UN Security Council's permanent seat offer that came to India, to China, nor on the sudden ceasefire in the 1948 Indo-Pak war that gave away POK.

Such innumerable hitherto hidden facts and truths came into the open through social media.

This "selective Sociology and History" was made bare post-2014, and this led to more and more Hindus and nationalists getting to know the real history, which further alienated the Congress.

 Factor 6: Modi fits the bill as " The PM Hindus/Indians long waited for", and as the one who fulfilled their key demands and exceeded their expectations.

Remember the BJP's Mission- "Hindu-centric, resurgent and developed Bharat as Vishwaguru"

Every step and act of Modi, during the first two terms as PM, has been moving towards these three key objectives of the Mission BJP.

A FEW EXAMPLES OF HINDU-CENTRIC ACTS:

- Modi is genuinely very proud as a Hindu. He follows all traditions and customs as a devout

Hindu. But the biggest change he brought in politics is that he flaunted it and mainstreamed Hinduism.

- He started taking Hindu/Indian culture/ concepts such as yoga globally. He made the UN adopt a Yoga Day. Ayurveda has got a fillip.
- Most importantly, he fulfilled the long-pending demand of a grand Prabhu Sri Ram Mandir at Ayodhya.
- The abrogation of Article 370 is also considered a victory for the Hindus.
- A bold move to accommodate the Hindus, Sikhs, and other minorities subjugated in the neighboring Islamic countries through CAA.
- Putting Hindi on the global stage.

A FEW EXAMPLES OF "RESURGENT INDIA" RELATED ACTS:

- Modi's " foreign affairs and diplomacy credentials" were often questioned before his ascent as PM. He has done amazingly well on this front and has put India on a pedestal as a global power.
- India-advantage independent foreign policy is the hallmark of Modi's era. Import of oil from Russia during the Ukraine war amidst the opposition of the West is the best example.
- Successful conduct of G-20 Presidency in India, and the Vishwaguru approach by bringing the African Union into G-20.
- Increased importance to "Climate Change" and renewable energy and taking its leadership at the global level.

- Leadership of the global south.
- Successful COVID vaccine diplomacy
- Tens of cases of successful eviction of Indians and other nationalities from conflict zones.
- "Disaster relief support" across the globe.
- Showcasing India's overall progress to the world through "indigenous COVID vaccine" and "Chandrayaan II" etc.

A FEW EXAMPLES OF "STRONG INDIA":

- The Balakot air strike sent a strong message to Pakistan and the world that India will strike back and big if someone meddles with it.
- The Galwan clash with the Chinese soldiers and the deployments at the borders made it amply clear that India shall not tolerate China's "big brother and belligerent" approach.
- Maldives' new regime exhibited its pro-China stance. Modi silently established Lakshadweep as an alternative tourist destination and also a new naval base in a month.
- Srilanka's Rajapakse government was pro-China. But he was made to realize it was India who would be its genuine brother by extending all unconditional support when it was on the brink of economic collapse.
- Induction of most advanced fighter jets, ships, and armaments, and providing the best of the suits and gears to the defense personnel.

RAJA DHARMA:

- The better the people, the better it is to garner votes. Modi is a master strategist and also the one who genuinely wants to uplift the lives of the masses and reduce their burden.
- All the government programs and beneficiaries are very much inclusive.
- No Prime Minister would have dared to talk about the poor condition of sanitation and the lack of toilets in most rural households. He did it in his very first Independence Day speech and brought new consciousness among the Indians about " Swacch Bharat".
- *Pucca* houses for crores of poor people.
- Free Ayushman Bharat to crores of people.
- Free ration to 80 crore members.
- National Educational Policy.
- Successful Direct Cash Transfer to crores of beneficiaries, checking middlemen menace and corruption.

ECONOMIC ACCOMPLISHMENTS:

- Coming out of "fragile five" economies.
- The fastest-growing large economy in the world.
- The fifth largest economy in the world.
- Transforming from a cash/black/ informal economy to a formal economy.
- "One Nation One Tax" in the form of GST.
- Unbelievable progress in infrastructure and logistics.

- Tremendous vision of BHIM UPI and its phenomenal success.
- Streamlining of the banking systems.
- Making PSUs competent.
- Extra emphasis on building the manufacturing sector.
- Scamfree administration.
- Stopping middlemen and lobbyists.
- Emphasis on start-up movement and improvement in start-up ecosystem and support.
- Even a simple thing such as the government-to-government purchase of urea and coating it with neem so that it is not diverted to chemical factories has saved hundreds of crores of rupees and has eliminated the shortage of fertilizers so vital to agriculture.

>>>

**Why MODI** IS *NUMERO UNO!*

**SanKaLP**- Skills, Knowledge, Leadership & Persona, is what I use to assess someone, more so, a leader. It's very tough to develop, hone, and become the best in terms of Skills, Knowledge, Leadership, and Persona and one needs a firm resolve (Sankalp) to master them. Hence, I have termed it SanKaLP.

What does any voter expect from someone to be their best Prime Minister?

Based on this SanKaLP model from 0-10 scale, if anyone assesses Narendra Modi and simultaneously, prominent leaders in the Opposition such as Rahul Gandhi, Arvind

Kejriwal, Mallikarjuna Kharge or Mamata Banerjee, and even other leaders in the BJP and NDA such as Amit Shah, Yogi Adityanath, Dr. Jaishankar, Nitish Kumar, it shall become clear why Modi is real *numero uno.*

"Leadership is a process of self-development, says an article by Harvard Business Review. "No one can *teach* you how to lead; you need to be willing and able to *learn* how to lead. Mostly we learn from our experiences and facing adversity. Stepping outside of the spaces where we feel safe — is a powerful teacher."

ADVERSITY is indeed the most powerful teacher. Modi faced a string of adversities in the beginning years of his political career. A deep thinker, a quick learner, and adaptable Modi is, he successfully overcame those adversities, kept working harder and harder, and continually reformed and unbelievably transformed himself.

According to that HBR article, these are the top eight most important qualities for successful leadership:

**1. Authenticity**

"Being genuine is fundamental to success in any role. As a leader, you must embody your best self — the version that's not only highly effective but also capable of motivating and inspiring those around you"."Your competence is not enough; people need to trust your character and connect with you, otherwise they will not be willing to take risks with you," the article says.

Going by the main points of this key attribute, Modi is effective, inspires others, and gains the full trust of his teammates, hence they risk everything with him.

## 2. Curiosity

"Curiosity is a mindset: "It's about looking around the corner, exploring uncharted territories, and trying to understand the art of the possible." Great leaders have an "outside-in" perspective of their organizations and teams. This means they can look at situations and issues from the standpoint of external stakeholders, such as customers or competitors. This helps them make more informed decisions because they consider the broader context, beyond just internal organizational dynamics."

In an interaction with children once, when a child was explaining something interesting, Modi asked, " *kaise karte hain aap*".

On many occasions, he has expressed surprise at the creative prowess of common people on social media.

It's his curiosity backed with determination and execution ability that could find a solution to many situations such as the Balakot strike or COVID.

## 3. Analytical prowess

"Leadership requires the ability to break down complex problems, identify their root causes, and come up with fresh solutions. Trusting your gut will not suffice. Instead, you need to develop your analytical skills by focusing on cause-and-effect relationships and being attentive to patterns and trends"

"Making sound decisions hinges on your ability to leverage your experience along with a blend of analytics, expertise, and ethical judgment, While being data-savvy is paramount for leaders, "it's not about being data-driven, it's about being data-informed."

Modi's big decisions such as GST, demonetization that resulted in the digital payment revolution, abrogation of Article 370 and grand Sri Ram Mandir at Ayodhya without hiss, replacing the entire Gujarat cabinet on the eve of the Assembly elections and winning with the biggest margin, etc stand testimony to his analytical prowess.

## 4. Adaptability

"The world is changing faster than it used to in part because of emerging technology and artificial intelligence. As a result, "stakeholder expectations are evolving faster and you, as a leader, need to be able to adjust to these ever-shifting demands" the HBR article says. It also says, "Adaptability fosters an agile team culture. It allows you to be able to swiftly respond to different dynamics, pivot when needed, and embrace new opportunities and challenges".

Modi keeps using "Tradition with Technology". Right from his days as the Chief Minister, he has been very open and adaptable and is also adept at adopting the right technology to find solutions to various socio-economic issues.

The best case study of Modi's adaptability could be seen at the time of COVID. During the initial onslaught of COVID, India virtually had nothing including basics such as masks and PPE kits, later oxygen, beds, vaccines, etc. He showed dexterity and adaptability and could control COVID in a massive nation like India, better and faster any other nation in the world.

## .5. Creativity

"Any idea that is new and useful to the organization is creativity. "Some of those ideas are incremental and others are breakthroughs."

Aadhaar is one of the biggest achievements of the Congress-led UPA government. The telecom revolution happened during Rajiv Gandhi's period. But making the best use of them to get solutions to people's day-to-day lives is Modi's creativity. UPI revolution is something the world is amazed with. Coating urea with neem so that it is not "misused" by diverting it to the chemical factories, utilizing waterways for easier mass transportation, light-weight train bodies, etc are samples of his creative solutions.

## 6. Comfort with ambiguity

"Managing ambiguity is about holding conflicting ideas in your head and dealing with competing priorities that feel equally important, says Hill. Many people fall into the trap of linear thinking, believing that X causes Y, and as a result, they may overlook the interplay of different dynamics. To be an effective leader, you need to cultivate a systems mindset, "which helps you understand how things are connected and allows you to grapple with opposing ideas in the face of uncertainty." But at times, you might still feel as though you're "navigating through a fog."

Imagine Modi on the eve of demonetization or the Balakot air strike or abrogation of Article 370 and how many "what ifs or "what if not" he must have posed his team and himself and how he would have cruised over those uncertain, ambiguous outcomes, and still made the right decisions.

## 7. Resilience

"Charging ahead with unwavering vision can spell trouble in today's dynamic and competitive environment. Successful leaders recognize the fluid nature of situations and strive to understand the cultural context within which they operate. Most important, they exhibit the resilience to recalibrate if they're veering off course. "You need to know how to regroup and get input from others by asking, 'Is there another path?'"

One of the first enactments he brought after becoming the Prime Minister in his first term was the Land Acquisition Bill. It caused uproar. Without any rigidity, he withdrew.

During Barack Obama's visit as a special guest for India's Republic Day, Modi wore his name-embroidered costly suit gifted by an admirer. The Indian people were upset. He immediately put the suit on auction and gifted that money to a social cause.

Immediately after his thumping victory, the BJP lost very badly in the Delhi Assembly elections and the Bihar Assembly elections. So with Rajasthan, Madhya Pradesh and Chattisgarh Assembly elections just before the 2019 Lok Sabha elections.

During the initial days of COVID, and later, he was put to severe tests including an emergency nationwide lockdown for which he was widely condemned. Even his long beard which was left uncut during the COVID's dark days was ridiculed though it is said that he was doing some penance to get rid of the dread at the earliest.

He exhibited extraordinary resilience in all challenging situations and overcame everything to stupendous success.

## 8. Empathy

"Understanding and connecting with others on an emotional level is a key trait of strong leadership. Leaders must foster relationships, build trust, and actively engage with their team members. You need to be able to step into the shoes of your team members, understand what matters to them, what their priorities are, and identify common ground. Developing your emotional intelligence gives you a deeper appreciation of the complex challenges others are working through, and helps you foster a more supportive and nurturing environment".

One might recall an occasion when Modi washed the feet of *karmacharis*. On every momentous occasion including the inauguration of a marvellous new Parliament building, he showed special gestures towards those *karmachari*s.

Though he doesn't express emotions, he seems high on emotional intelligence as he senses what the people need and has come out with holistic and unique programs benefiting them.

His top team is a well-knit, cohesive team. If Modi didn't understand his teammates and their needs and didn't accommodate them, the team would not have been so loyal and committed.

Empathy needs to be differentiated from sympathy. He seems to have both for the people and his team. But, it is beyond doubt that he doesn't have empathy or sympathy toward his archrivals in the country or outside the country.

>>>

**What makes a good political leader?**

The Bangalore Political Action Committee (B.PAC.) lists the following attributes that make someone a good political leader:

1.  Man with a vision and purpose

2.  Honesty and Integrity

3.  Decisive ( or decision-making ability)

4.  Must be able to inspire others

5.  Good communicator

6.  Must delegate tasks effectively

Quite several examples have been provided in the preceding pages, and the people are well aware of various incidents, developments, and Modi's actions and decisions. On each of the six attributes listed by B. PAC., Modi stands out *vis-à-vis* all other leaders in the Opposition as well as within the BJP/NDA which makes him *numero uno* political leader in this vast country.

>>>

## 2024-34: Modi moving towards becoming Mahaan!?

**The 2024** Lok Sabha elections are underway, and their results are a foregone conclusion. Modi shall be back as the Prime Minister for the third consecutive term.

The key question in this term is, as per the BJP's party constitution, whoever turns 75 shall have to vacate an active political role. Modi shall turn 75 in 2026 but he shall be asked not to vacate, by the party as well as the voters, and he may not, as some tasks are to be fulfilled as yet and it would take up two more terms till 2034.

Having cleaned up the system in the first term, Modi wanted to pace things during the second term but COVID came as a spoiler. Yet he has managed to fulfill key promises of the BJP- abrogation of Article 370, the opening of the grand Sri Ram Mandir at Ayodhya, and the Uniform Civil Code (UCC) being implemented at the state level. The Citizenship Amendment Act (CAA) that provides citizenship to the " subjugated Hindus and Sikhs" in neighboring Muslim-dominated countries is a bonus.

He has already set the tone about some things to come, during his third term but having studied Modi for over 25 years, I have something more- untold by him or anyone- to "unveil" many more things on the anvil, during his third and fourth term.

1. In his fourth term, he shall break the record of Nehru's longest-serving Prime Minister.
2. Bringing the BJP to power in all state assemblies Having brought his party to power in most states, West Bengal, Kerala, and Tamil Nadu are the key states he would like to put his party/ coalition in power sooner or later.

Assam has close to 40% of the Muslim population, still, the BJP has managed to capture power in the state and also win the high number of MP seats. West Bengal has 30% of the Muslim population. So, the BJP can gain power. But the leader of the Opposition, Trinamool's Mamata Banerjee is quite fierce there. The BJP has already made incredible inroads in the state during the past five years. Besides, there's another quite influential party in the form of CPIM which is ideologically opposite to Mamata which might cut into the votes of the Opposition. So, sooner or later, West Bengal shall be won by the BJP.

Kerala is already opening up to the BJP. Kerala has 55% Hindu, 27% Muslim and 18% Christian population. Kerala has the Left-led coalition and

Congress-led coalition as two main political blocks. Wherever just one political block is very dominant, the BJP has been successful in making inroads. It will be an interesting watch but the trends are that the Hindus are consolidating and there's a better understanding of what's happening between the Hindus and Christians as in Goa. Once the BJP builds strong leadership at the state level, the voters might shift to the BJP.

Tamil Nadu is the southernmost state of India. It's in Kanya Kumari, the southernmost tip, Swami Vivekananda meditated for three days nonstop on a sea rock and saw the vision of "one India". Tamil Nadu is the only state in India that has a religious symbol- temple gopuram, as its state emblem. Still, it is in this state that anti-Hindu and anti-Hindi agitations happened the most.

Modi is well aware of the fact that he has to reach out more in this state to win over. Modi- Xi Ping second informal summit happened at Mamallapuram. The Hindu sacred Sengol from Tamil Nadu was installed at the new Parliament building. Most importantly, he has installed a young, dynamic ex-IPS officer Annamalai as the state BJP President. This is the first time Hinduism is being taken into the political ground effectively by anyone in Tamil Nadu backed by development and economic agenda. The space occupied by the main block AIADMK is shrinking. If the current momentum created by the BJP state leadership is sustained, it's just a matter of time.

Jammu & Kashmir is one small state that the BJP doesn't ignore due to its strategic significance. With it becoming a Union Territory after the abrogation of Article 370, development initiatives of the BJP and an increase in tourists are being appreciated by the locals. With the delimitation of state Assembly seats underway, the number of seats in the Jammu region, where the Hindus are dominant, shall increase and neutralize the advantage the Opposition parties had or tilt the balance in the BJP's favor. So, J & K shall also follow suit.

3. "Congress-*mukt*" Bharat

India's oldest political party is not just opposed but virtually hated by the BJP and Modi. The Congress which always revolved around the Gandhi family, has already become "Gandhi-*mukt*" Congress with a non-Gandhi being its President.

The Congress getting any power at the Centre soon seems impossible. It seems Rahul Gandhi is fighting his best during the 2024 Lok Sabha elections. In case he loses and loses badly, there's a possibility of him exiting active politics. After the debacle in 2019, he resigned from the Congress's Presidentship. Something more might happen after the 2024 Lok Sabha elections. It's quite natural that he would be badly demoralized and dejected after having lost three straight elections.

The Congress is surviving in very few states based on the state leadership. The prominent of those states are Karnataka and Telangana. In Karnataka,

Siddaramaiah is the real vote-getter for the Congress and he will not contest any more elections. The BJP lost the last elections by a whisker and by its own mistakes. JDS is a coalition partner of the BJP currently. In the next Assembly elections, the Congress shall be on a weak wicket.

In Telangana, Chief Minister Revanth Reddy won due to anti-Bharat Rashtra Samiti votes. The BJP is already on the rise in this state. Revanth, anyway, is from the BJP's student wing Akhila Bharatiya Vidyarthi Parishad (ABVP) and recently called Modi "his elder brother". Already, there are rumors that he might join hands with the BJP after the Lok Sabha elections and form a new government. No surprise if it happens or on the eve of the next Assembly elections as anyway the BJP is on the rise in the state..

This leaves the Congress as a minor partner in two states- Tamil Nadu and Jharkhand. At the most, it appears the regional satraps of the Congress will become splinter groups and the Congress will lose whatever significance it is left with.

4. Women's Reservation Bill to be implemented which shall change the political landscape.

5. "One Nation One Election" to be implemented which shall reduce the burden on the exchequer, give ample scope to development activities and drastically reduce "political expenses" and thus, corruption.

6. To ensure victory and gain power, the BJP has compromised by giving tickets to some tainted politicians. However, that will stop, and "political cleansing" will begin.

7. Reducing dependence on caste lines in politics and emphasis on merits in the candidates' selection.

8. Delimitation of MP and MLA seats across the country that would raise the number of elected representatives.

9. Weakened political opposition.

10. Modi is aware there's still corruption at various levels. He shall take severe measures to curb or eliminate it.

11. Possibly, change the name of the country from India to Bharat. Currently, the Constitution says, "India, that is, Bharat". Just "India" might get deleted and deleted forever.

12. India become a permanent member of the all-important United Nations Security Council and possibly have a Secretary General of the UN.

13. The world's third largest economy.

14. Fast-paced overall economic development, making India the third-largest economy.

15. Extra emphasis on building world-class infrastructure and supply chain and boosting the manufacturing sector, creating more employment.

16. Precedence to socio-economic development rather than religious aspects.

17. Greater emphasis on ease of living and implementation of "citizen's holistic, integrated development plan".

18. Emphasis on " All are Indians, and all Indians are one" thus, making nationalism and collective progress the main agenda and reducing or eliminating the fissures between religious communities.

19. Unveiling of a mega, long-term, and transformative pan-India project such as the interlinking of rivers.
20. Making India on par with the best in the world in terms of progress in Science & Technology.

21. Keeping the Indian military "always advanced, alert, agile and able" and borders safe and secure.

22. Possibly, the people of Pakistan-occupied Kashmir aspire to become a part of India and could be integrated.

23. Staying neutral and playing a proactive role in the world order, focusing more on the environment, climate, renewable energy, and world peace.

Ram Rajya is what we have heard of. That's an ideal, utopian state and impossible to realize in this modern, complex era. Modi might redefine some things and bring in a new dimension that could be termed " Modi Rajya" and could set a new template for the world.

**If all the above happens, what will stop Bharat from becoming Vishwaguru? And Modi from becoming Mahaan?**